July 4

Court TV 20.2

To my children three: Jack, Leora and Loren,
and their spouses: Fern Fisher, Tim Duch
and Joe Berlinger.

For my stakes in posterity:
    Julia, Reva and Bennett Eiferman,
    Nicholas and Jonah Duch and
    Sarah and Maya Berlinger.

IT'S TIME

Yep, it's time. Time for what? Well, this is how the following sort of got underway. I received a phone call from my daughter Leora the other morning and she said "It's time Mom, time to write an autobiography". Her words hung between a suggestion and a request. I probably am responding to both.

What motivated this? Some time ago we celebrated my 90th birthday. I still can't believe it's true. It was a lovely celebration with almost the entire immediate family and a few chosen friends. I have been on a "high" ever since. I guess events such as these give birth to memories and perspective. As a writer, Leora, aware of the timing, placed her suggestion into the hopper.

Where to begin? If I start with "me" a lot of history will be missing. Do I have a responsibility to transmit some presence of the past? If I am going to embark on this venture, I guess I do. I'll therefore attempt to record some of the information about the family before my time, which I remember, or was transmitted to me by others. Since I have outlived every one of my generational immediate relatives, here are some of the tales I was told.

TALES I WAS TOLD

By the way, I admire alliteration and even though it is sometimes corny and/or contrived, I tend to use it.

Paternal Pictures: One of the things I was told was that the family name "Berlinger" was originally "Beadak". There are conflicting stories about the surname. One is that the three sons, Abe, Louis and Mendel who came to the States, came via Berlin and thus Berlinger was the assigned surname. Or the famous or infamous immigration clerk on Ellis Island changed Baedak to Berlinger. Or the name was Berlinger all along. Be that as it may, all of our relatives were Berlingers, no matter when they arrived on these shores or which immigration officer they encountered. One last story that I was told, was that prior to leaving Suwalki for these shores, they all changed their names from Baedak to Berlinger. When I asked what Baedak meant in Polish, I was told "poor man". No wonder they changed the name before leaving for the *gildinah medinah* (golden land)!

My grandfather's name was *Dov Baer*, in English, Benjamin David. He married my grandmother, *Runya Garbowsky*. They lived in an area which was alternately Russia and at other times Poland. I am

2

not sure which country it was when they lived there. I think it was Poland. The town or *shtetel* was called Suwalki. I remember the name because it's similar to a popular sandwich item sold in restaurants, consisting of chunks of fat and beef, shaved from a revolving cone called Suvlaki.

Suwalki

Bubby Runya

They had four sons and a daughter, Abe, Louis, Mendel, Jack and Ida. My father Jack was the youngest. The family was comfortable and in Europe, they owned the equivalent of a small grocery store or bodega. They had hired help, but the "establishment" was supervised by my grandmother. My grandfather supplied provisions, clothing and food, to the Russian army. This was probably the primary source of the family's income. The three older boys went to America, possibly to avoid conscription into service. Ida was sent to the States sometime after, in order to presumably put an end to a love affair. Abe went into jewelry manufacturing in lower Manhattan. The business prospered. In Europe, Abe and possibly Louis as well, had apprenticed as goldsmiths. My father Jack was 14 when he and his parents emigrated to the United States. They arrived on June 8th 1910. My grandfather passed away in 1918.

My father went to school in the U.S. and then went into the jewelry business with his brother Abe. After a period of time, he left his brother and started his own business. He was a very gifted and talented designer of jewelry.

Abe and his family, as well as my grandmother, Bubby Runya, lived at 1336 53rd street in Borough Park, Brooklyn. It was a large, two family frame house, with an additional attic apartment and a wrap around front porch. Bubby Runya lived in the attic apartment. What a *schlepp* (drag) that must have been! After they were married, my father and mother lived on the ground floor. But I'm getting ahead of the sequence of events.

Much of what I am writing about is just a listing of facts, dates and events as I remember them being related to me. I cannot vouch for their accuracy. They are veiled by time and memory.

I recall the names of some relatives. Uncle Abe was married to aunt Bessie. They had four children,

Aaron, Milton, Roslyn and Dorothy. My uncle Lou was married to aunt Matilda. They had two daughters, Florence and Dorothy. They lived in Queens. When I was younger we kept in touch with them. My uncle Mendel was married to aunt Rosie. They had two children, Ralph and Beatrice. I recall Beatrice was my most "beautiful blonde cousin". Uncle Mendel had a commission bakery on Franklin Avenue in Brooklyn, near Ebbets Field.

An addition to what I remember about Berlinger genealogy and history: My father's sister Ida, married a "yankee", Samuel Myer Jr. They lived in Poughkeepsie, N.Y. They had three children: Helen, Ruth and Donald (Donnie). We remained very close to aunt Ida and her family. I remember Donnie as a brilliant, blond, young cousin. Donnie died shortly after his Bar Mitzvah from adolescent diabetes, which was not diagnosed in time.

Maternal Material: My grandfather's name was William, (*Z'eev Vulff*) Moser. He was a *Kohan*. The Mosers were the only Jewish family in Spring Valley, N.Y. at that time. How different it is today! I was told that my grandfather was born in Germany. He was married to a woman who died in childbirth in the U.S. They had four sons, Paul, Leo, Jack and David. He was a jeweler. He later married my maternal grandmother, Fanny Goldberg. I understand she originally came from France. In 1903 she gave birth to a baby girl weighing one and a half pounds! This was before incubators. The baby was kept wrapped in cotton batting. We were told that baby Frieda, my mother, was the size of a spring chicken. What a lovely spring chicken she turned out to be! A few years later my grandmother, Fanny, gave birth to my twin uncles, Henry and Sammy. So now there were six boys and a girl in the family! It was a large, loving family.

Bubby Fanny (middle) and Zeyda
Spring Valley House

The older boys left home, Spring Valley, early on. David went into the service. He died in France during WWI. I think he was killed not by the Germans, but in the influenza virus epidemic. Leo died of diabetes some years later. Paul went to Hollywood and was featured as the cowboy "Paul Mix". When he came East to visit us, he always entertained us with his rope tricks. Uncle Jack was the first teacher of mechanical dentistry in the Board of Education of NYC. I seem to remember that he was the one who introduced the course into the city's trade school curriculum. He was married to aunt Ruth. She rarely visited us, although we saw uncle Jack frequently. They had one daughter, Lucille.

Writing an autobiography is for some, or even many, a literary endeavor. I am finding it to be, at this point, a recording of names, events and dates, many of them not verifiable. It is both frustrating and painful that there isn't anyone left to "check the facts out". Had this project been undertaken in an earlier decade, it would have been fleshed out in a more interesting manner, rather than routine reporting.

Some of the stories about my mother's childhood include the following: When my mother was a baby, people didn't hire baby sitters, they just took the children with them, if there was no other option. My grandfather had a retail jewelry repair shop in town. He serviced Tuxedo Park, an area of very wealthy individuals. One of his customers was Mr. Harriman, the wealthy mogul. My grandfather had to deliver a piece of jewelry to him. No one was available to be with baby Frieda, so she went along with her daddy. Teddy Roosevelt was visiting the Harrimans at that time. He, T.R., was taken by the adorable baby girl, little Frieda. He kept bouncing her on his knee. He asked my grandfather to please bring little Frieda the next time he visited the Harrimans. Sometime later, the Harrimans informed my grandfather when Teddy Roosevelt was coming for another visit. My grandfather returned with his little girl. Teddy Roosevelt, once again, repeated how he was struck by the adorable little girl and said he had brought a gift for her! He gave my grandfather an 18 k gold ring in the shape of a snake with a tiny diamond as the eye, as a gift for Frieda. When I was 12 years old my mother gave me the ring as a *Bat Mitzvah* gift.

The Mosers lived in Spring Valley, New York, in a large, white, rambling farmhouse atop a hill called Slims Hill. Today the property and the hill are occupied by a hotel. Once, when my mother was about six or seven years old, she was playing near her house, fell and rolled down the embankment. She was badly bruised, and ended up with lock jaw. Today, we have an injection and antibiotics to prevent and cure the infection. It took a long time for her to recover.

My mother did not attend college. Her report cards from high school attest to her excellent academic achievements. She was brilliant in many ways. After high school graduation, she worked in the jewelry field. Part of her job entailed delivering jewelry. One of the deliveries was to my father's shop in the lower East Side in Manhattan and the rest is our history. They fell in love.

Frieda Moser   *Jacob (Jack) Berlinger*

When my mother was engaged she was 18 years old. My father fashioned a platinum engagement ring with nine filigreed flowers on each side, to coincide with her age He set a small diamond in each flower and a rose cut, large, perfect diamond in the center. He knew she loved chocolate. If there was a foil wrapped chocolate in the center of the candy box, she would always go for it. He planned his proposal. He bought a box of Whitman's chocolates, hollowed out the center foil wrapped one and placed the engagement ring in it. She went for it! No, she did not break her tooth. They were engaged. A wedding subsequently followed. After they were married they moved into the ground floor of the house in Borough Park.

Freda Moser Berlinger and Jacob (Jack) Berlinger,
1922

My grandfather, William, had a stroke which left him paralyzed on his left side. I seem to recall that it was said that he had the stroke some time after he was told that his son David died overseas. Fanny, my grandmother, cared for my grandfather at the farmhouse until she died. After that, my grandfather came to live with us. We called him *Zayde*. I don't know if there were nursing homes available at that time. Even if they were, I am sure our family would prefer to care for their own at home. My mother then became the caregiver for her father. I remember Zayde as an avuncular, short man who pushed an armless, wooden, kitchen chair to navigate. The chair had no wheels and we knew he was coming into the room when we heard the soft scratching of the chair. Although he couldn't speak, his presence was pleasant and non intrusive. He was a sweet, quiet, stocky person. I remember the feel of his scratchy chin when I kissed him good night. His verbal communication was limited, since speech was an ability he lost when he had the stroke. Despite that, Zayde was nice to have around. We missed him when he died.

As I write this autobiography, the contents of my memory clustered in my skull, feel like a tea ball, filtered and censored by ego and diluted by time. Instead of organizing this material chronologically, I'm writing or recording fragments as I dig them out of my memory bank. That being said, I've reached my *beraycheet* (beginning).

MY BIRTH

Bells were ringing, everyone, everyone was celebrating. It was New Year's Eve 1923! I was the first baby born in the United States that year! The front page of a newspaper, which I think was called the Journal American (but I'm not sure), so stated. I no longer have a copy, but there was a photograph of my mother, me and Dr. Minenberg, the obstetrician, accompanying the article. The headline in the newspaper declared that "Women Will Rule This Year". It was my first feminist act. Several other newspapers made note of "the event", including the New York Times. There were no computers to validate the happening. I was it!

GIRL BORN ON STROKE OF 12.

Brooklyn Parents Lay Claim to New Year's Baby.

Just as the whistles, horns, sirens and bells blared the first minute of the New Year last night a baby girl was born in the Borough Park Maternity Hospital at Forty-sixth Street and Fifteenth Avenue, Brooklyn.

The parents are Mr. and Mrs. Jacob Berlinger of 1,836 Fifty-third Street, Brooklyn. The physician was Dr. Philip Mininberg. N.Y. Times Pg. 15

First News of The New Year

12 P. M.—A baby girl was born to Mrs. Jacob Berlinger of No. 1336 53d Street, Brooklyn, at the Borough Park Maternity Hospital, 45th Street and 15th Avenue Brooklyn. The World Pg. 1

NY Times pg. 15 - 1/1/23   The World pg. 1 - 1/1/23

I understand that my mother was preparing several ducks for a New Year's Eve party that evening and with no freezers available at the time, the ducks were given away. As a postscript: I was told that Dr. Minenberg had so much positive publicity with my birth that he subsequently opened a maternity hospital in Borough Park bearing his name. Recently, in preparing some remarks for my 90th birthday celebration, I Googled the Dr., and sure enough, he did open the maternity hospital and it lasted 40 years.

Deborah at 6 months

I am told that I was named "Doris Bernice Berlinger". However I can only remember being called "Deborah". All my school records and official documents, have Deborah as my first name. I do have one memory of my little sister, Evelyn, crying or rather complaining, to my mother, "Das no play leiree". Whether I was called "Doris", or whether "Das" was Evie's name for me, I don't know.

As an aside, "leiree" referred to a ball game we

13

played. One chanted "One, two, three aleiree, I spy mistress Saree, sitting on a bumble lairee, just like a chocolate fairy". As one bounced a pink rubber ball on the rhyming word, the bouncer waved her leg over the ball. If one missed waving her leg, or the ball double bounced, "you were out", and the next girl had her turn. Bouncing ball games were played primarily by girls.

We lived in the house in Borough Park for the first few years of my life. My sister Evelyn was born on December 29, 1925, while we still lived there. The house was near the synagogue, *Shomrei Emunah*, which my Bubby Runyah religiously and consistently attended. Some *Shabbos* (Sabbath) mornings I accompanied her. It was a treat. The synagogue was the biggest building I ever saw. It had so many steps, I first thought they led to heaven! I think Bubby Runya enjoyed my company those mornings as much as I felt privileged to accompany her. My infant sister Evie and I were the youngest grandchildren living in the big house and probably that is what enhanced our relationship with Bubby.

I remember sitting on Bubby's lap in the attic. The sun was shining through the windows. Bubby, frequently speaking Yiddish, would show me her jewelry. (Her sons were in the business). She knew I loved looking at and admiring those lovely items. Bubby held up a diamond studded, heart pendant

14

and twirled the chain it hung on in the sunshine. The rainbows it formed, swirled around us. She knew I loved watching this magical display. She said to me in English, "Devoralah, someday this will be yours." And we played on. More on this heartwarming experience later on.

I haven't used the limited Yiddish words I knew for decades. Oddly enough, as I write about my memories of Bubby in the attic, many forgotten words are coming back to me now, in my 90's!

Another Borough Park memory I have is the first purchase I made. My mother sent me to the store to buy two cents worth of soup greens. The two pennies were wrapped in brown paper, torn from a paper grocery bag. I held on to them tightly. The vegetable store was on 13th avenue, around the corner. I remember feeling so grown up and responsible. Unbeknownst to me, my mother was a few feet behind me all the way!

Evie was an adorable little girl. When she learned to walk, she was always at my side or behind me. Her skin was so white and soft, mother called her *Kotchkeleh*, (baby duckling). We later named her "Kotch", a nickname she never liked.

As a very young child I recall visiting maternal grandparents in Spring Valley, in their big white house. They had a small farm next to the house. Two cows supplied them with milk. I remember drinking the foamy warm milk which my Bubby Fanny just "squeezed out of the bottom of the cow"! She took care of the running of the farm while grandfather dealt with his jewelry business.

At one visit there was a large circle of straw in the middle of the kitchen floor. To my squealing delight, there was a whole cluster of pale, yellow, baby chicks running within the enclosure. This was in my grandparents' kitchen, not in a pet store! Bubby Fanny explained to me that the chicken house was too cold for the baby chicks. For breakfast in the morning, my Bubby gave me a raw, warm egg that she had just collected from the chickens. I guess salmonella was not a risk factor in those days. Bubby Fanny was the one who arranged for the *shochet* (an itinerant individual who slaughtered the fowl according to Jewish dietary rules) to come when needed. I remember helping Bubby Fanny churn a wooden cask and watching the curds and whey separate and magically produce deep, yellow butter from cream! She was a small, thin woman, who performed magical things on that farm miles and years, far away and long ago. She died when I was about three or four years old. Both my maternal grandparents are buried in the old Jewish cemetery in Spring Valley.

I do not recall when we moved from Borough Park to Kensington. It was an area which bordered Borough Park and Midwood Manor. During the Depression, my uncle Mendel was having some financial difficulties and was facing foreclosure of his home. He sold the house to my father and we moved into 777 East 5th street. I loved our home and the address. I grew up there along with my two sisters.

Deborah Growing Up

THE DEPRESSION
AND DEPRIVATION

My entire childhood, except the first few years, was spent while we lived on East 5th street. My parents opened our home to relatives and assorted friends during the Depression. I do not remember any time during that period when we only had our nuclear family living at home. Initially, my maternal grandfather lived with us during his post-stroke period. Next, my paternal grandmother decided not to live alone and chose to live with us on East 5th street. She was with us until she passed away in 1933, shortly before my baby sister Ronya was born. While my father was sitting *shiva* for his mother, my baby sister was born on March 28, 1933 and was named Ronya after our grandmother, Runya.

Another resident in our home was a young neighbor, a friend of my mother. I do not recall her name. She lived with us for several months and I was told to keep it a secret. She rarely went outdoors, except occasionally at night. At the time that she lived with us I did not know or understand the dynamics surrounding her residency. The mystery was solved years later when I learned that she had been pregnant. Having a child out of wedlock was frowned upon and a source of shame for a family. Her parents would have been devastated if they knew her situation. She turned to my mother for help. My young mother offered her a home, when her out-of-wedlock pregnancy was becoming obvious. She was a plump, twenty year old. It was decided she would move literally up the block into our apartment without her family or anyone else knowing. She told everyone that she was moving away. Both she and the father of the baby had wanted to get married, but during the Depression they couldn't afford the expense. Abortion was an option which was never considered. The story has a happy ending. The couple married, she gave birth to a baby girl, where or when I do not know, and they "lived happily ever after".

As a baby and well into her first year, Ronya was an avid "thumbsucker". The latest "cure" was perforated aluminum cups with attachments of cheese cloth and strings. Her tiny hands were completely ensconced in the aluminum restraints. I always thought it was cruel. However, it was the latest recommendation by the medical "experts". It's a wonder that she matured into a normal, outgoing, loving woman. Evie and I were thrilled to have a baby girl as part of the family. We doted on her every developmental stage.

Other residents in our home through the years, included my two cousins, Helen and Ruth Myer from Poughkeepsie, the daughters of my father's sister, Ida. Each cousin lived with us for the full four years, not concurrently, while they attended Hunter College. Hunter is a public college and at the time was tuition-free for New York City residents. The cousins were about 10 years or so older than me, and were like my older sisters. We always had a close relationship. My mother periodically would assist them academically. To my amazement, I never understood how she could do it, never having attended college herself.

Cousin Helen Myer   Cousin Ruth Myer

My mother's twin brothers were always close to the family, especially Henry. When we were very young, my sister Evie and I received a life sized doll, as a gift from them. The doll had a soft fabric body and a beautiful porcelain face with eyes that opened and closed. We named it after our uncles, Henry and Samuel Moser, "Henrietta Samuella Mosietta

Berlinger". Whenever we played, we always called the doll by the full name, "Henrietta, Samuella Mosietta". Uncle Henry was particularly devoted and fond of us. He had been married and subsequently divorced, and never had any children of his own. We were his substitute children. When we were older, he bought us our first "two wheeler". It was a shiny, beautiful, red bike that I learned to ride, but always had a problem stopping!

I remember how excited Henry, my mother and father were when Henry, a taxi driver, purchased his medallion. It was very expensive at the time, and still is. It was a major investment, and the family celebrated Henry's reaching a status in life, especially during the Depression.

I recall accompanying my mother once on a Friday, when she asked our tenant to help her, by accepting an extra chicken that she claimed was delivered by mistake for *Shabbos*. When we got back upstairs to our apartment I asked my mother to explain what she did. She answered, "*Devoraleh*",(the diminutive of my Hebrew name which she frequently and affectionately called me) "when you give *tsadakah* (a form of charity) you should not embarrass the recipient, you should make them think **they** are doing a good deed by helping **you**". This was typical of my mother. She never passed a panhandler without leaving a contribution. She left, by her actions, a heritage of values for us, my sisters and me, to live by.

Summers on East 5th street were a busy and happy time. As children, we played and created games of diversion and frequently friendly competition. We played "stoop ball", throwing a small rubber ball against the brick steps and depending on where the ball landed and how many bounces before we retrieved it, the players scored. Those games kept us busy for hours and days. We played jump rope, "immies" (beautiful little globes of glass) or marbles, that were aimed at an area on the ground. We played "Hi-Li", a wooden paddle attached to a long rubber band and a very small rubber ball at the end. Depending upon how many times one could consistently hit the bouncing ball with the paddle, one scored. We played with yo-yo's, with metal jacks, and card games. We sewed and embroidered patterns on squares of canvas. We drew and cut paper dolls, making elaborate outfits for them and traveled the world with them.

Another one of my favorite games was "vegetable store". The vegetables were the available back yard weeds which we harvested. Plantain, giant foxtail and broadleaf dock were favorites. As the weeds matured and summer waned, we used the spikes and seed stalks, stripping some of them. Dandelions, lamb's quarters, and common ragweed at different stages, filled our larder. Curley dock was a perfect substitute for parsley. We occasionally used parts of milkweed. The shopping lists were as creative as the green selection. We made our own paper money and the riches of East 5th street were in the control and in the hands of its underage inhabitants. We read many books, not by request or necessity, but because we wanted to! Those summers were great. We played outdoors, weather permitting, all day long. There was no sleep-away camp or day camp or day trips or "play dates". No TV, just creative child's play abounded.

Names elude me, but I do recall the names of some of our playmates: Irwin Lubin, Marion Prisament, Bernice Brand, Samuel Sternberg and Norma Davidson. How come? There are times now when the name of someone I met recently eludes me, yet I can recall the names of children I played with 85 years ago! I can't fathom why I remember some facts and not others. It's a puzzlement.

New Years Eve has always been celebrated with the whole family together, since it is my birthday. When we were young, on New Year's Eve, we went to bed at our regular bedtime hour. Shortly before midnight, my parents would wake us up for the celebration. At that point we would greet the New Year with noisemakers, party hats, ice cream and a birthday cake.

When I was about nine or maybe ten, I received one of my most memorable birthday gifts. For a long time, I had said that someday I would love to have a white silk rain cape. When I was given a big box containing my birthday present, at midnight, I couldn't imagine what incredible contents were contained within. I opened the box and there was my dream come true. Lustrous white silk, sprinkled with a hundred shiny new copper pennies! I ecstatically picked it up, shook it and a copper profusion of coins showered down. It was magical!

HOT RED PERIL

Before my sister Ronya was born, I came down with scarlet fever, a serious childhood disease at that time. An official Department of Health representative placed a quarantine on our home. A placard was placed on my bedroom door and everyone was barred from entering except my mother, my caregiver. Each time she entered and after she left the room, she changed her clothing and washed her hands in a Lysol solution! I remember how red and irritated her hands were. No rubber or latex gloves were available yet. I was not hospitalized and remained at home. I missed the family. I was confined to one room, since I was seriously ill with a very high fever. At one time, fortunately, when Dr. Goodfellow (an apt name for a pediatrician) was examining me, I was told that my heart stopped beating. He revived me with an injection of adrenalin, which he said he always carried in case of an emergency. I do recall the dream I had then. I remember dreaming that I was being hurled through a tunnel with a bright light up ahead, at the tunnel's end. Today, the dream would probably be interpreted as a "near death experience".

My diet was restricted to soft and liquid. When I

started to return to a solid diet, my favorite dish was mashed potatoes wrapped in a lettuce leaf. When I recovered, everything I had handled had to be disinfected or fumigated, e.g. the set of the Book of Knowledge. The pages I read and reread were set out in the sunshine for hours, as well as all my toys, bedclothes, pajamas, etc. The period covering my illness and recovery lasted well over a month. My mother was complimented, in view of the fact that no one else in the family contracted scarlet fever.

ELEMENTARY SCHOOL

My mother explored and found a coed, Hebrew day school (yeshivah) that was just being established. It was the Yeshivah of Flatbush. She wanted her daughters to be educated in Judaism. This was way back in 1929! Evie and I attended and graduated from the Yeshivah of Flatbush. My sister Ronnie, who was 10 years younger than me, was also a graduate years later. The school had a dual curriculum. In the mornings, Monday to Thursday, there were Hebrew classes. We studied language, literature, history, Bible, Prophets and *Gemarah* (Talmud), all in the Hebrew language. In the afternoons, after lunch and recess, we covered the standard "English" curriculum. Friday, the order was reversed with English classes in the morning and Hebrew classes in the afternoon. We were taught the same subjects as the public schools, except in a three hour time span. Some of the extra-curricular subjects were thus eliminated or given token time, e.g. gym, music and art. On Fridays when we had the English program in the mornings we attended "assembly" as well. Friday we wore prescribed outfits. The girls wore navy skirts, white "middy" blouses and navy scarves. The boys wore dark knickers, white shirts and dark ties. Dress codes have certainly evolved since! However, in some parochial schools they are still mandated.

Deborah in Assembly Garb

The school was a Modern Orthodox yeshivah and I think was more liberal in its orientation and practices 80 years ago, than it is today. For example, the girls learned the *trop* (cantillation) and *Gemarah* (Talmud) along with the boys. We were able to chant the *parsha* (portion of the Bible). Not so today. Girls are no longer taught the cantillation. Some of the classes are not co-ed.

My mother felt that I should have a *Bat Mitzvah* celebration since I knew the portion but was prevented by law and custom from chanting it in the synagogue. Only boys had the privilege. Although it was not the custom in those days, I did chant the weekly portion in class. My mother brought soda and cookies for the class, as a symbol of the celebration. This was in 1935. She was a nascent feminist.

Most days we walked to school. It took about a half hour in good weather. At that time, there was no publicly subsidized school transportation. We did have the option to take the Coney Island Avenue trolley, which covered only half the trip. However, that cost five cents. In Depression years one dispensed with unnecessary expenditures.

Writing about the trip to school, I am reminded about my little sister, Ronnie, who walked to school alone, for about a year, just to save her trolley fare, ten cents a day for a round trip, so that she could buy me a graduation gift of a tennis racket! I kept that racket for years.

Attending a private school during the Depression involved tuition, which placed a strain on the family's financial resources. I recall that my father had to pay $30 a month per child and we had two in the Yeshivah at one time! I can just imagine how difficult it must have been for my parents to meet that obligation. I can never remember my mother ever buying a new winter coat. I do remember that, at one time, I only had two dresses for school. My mother would wash one, dry it by holding it out in front of the open grate of the basement furnace (the one that heated the house). There were no automatic washers and dryers in homes yet. When the dress was practically dry, she would iron it. That procedure was followed every few days. Many of the children in the school were from financially comfortable families. We were not. However, we always had more than adequate food. Compromises were made in the area of clothing. Today, when I look at my overflowing closet, with a wide selection of items, even in different sizes, I can't fathom the difference. I guess, having lived through the Depression, I find it difficult to dispose of usable items, even though they no longer fit me. I am under the impression or misimpression, that maybe, someday, I'll lose enough weight to fit into them again.

Graduation day from elementary school, the Yeshivah of Flatbush, was a painful one for me. I was to be the third honoree, one of three top students at the graduation ceremony. The first honoree was Jerome Robbins. More about Jerry later on. I don't remember who the second recipient was. On the morning of graduation day, Mar Rabinowitz took me aside. *"Mar"* was the Hebrew word for "Mister", the term we used in addressing the male faculty. He was an avuncular, large man, who was my favorite teacher. He took my hands between his enormous palms, gently informing me that there would be a change in the awards. Shifra's father was a large contributor, and was instrumental in the establishment of the school and therefore the third prize was to be awarded instead to Shifra that night. I was shocked and devastated. I burst out crying. Mar Rabinowitz tried to calm me and explained that we all knew that I deserved the award, but sometimes we have to make sacrifices to accommodate certain circumstances. I went home red eyed and miserable. Shifra was one of my best friends and she was bright. I didn't hold her responsible, nor did I resent her. We remained friends. I never told her about the award switch.

When I reached home, teary eyed, my mother tried to console me. I had decided that I would not attend graduation ceremonies. My mother, in her very special way, convinced me to go to graduation; I don't remember how. But, more importantly, she taught me how to cope with injustice and with unfortunate events. It took much more time for me to appreciate my mother's counsel and how to place experiences into perspective. That evening, I went to the graduation, respecting Mar Rabinowitz, still friendly with Shifra, and loving, but angry at my mother for convincing me to go. To this day, I remember how upset I was, whenever I saw the plaque with the three names carved on the old green wooden scroll and "Deborah Berlinger" not on it.

HIGH SCHOOLS AND SURGERIES

Erasmus Hall High School, in Brooklyn, was the first public school I attended. I found it challenging and a bit overwhelming in terms of its size. I did well academically and found the courses relatively easy. I was enrolled in a number of honor classes. One of my lifelong friendships was born in Erasmus. Selma Levine (later Zorn) lived on East 5th street near Cortelyou Road. We met at the bus stop and traveled to Erasmus and ongoing through life together for many years.

When I was about fourteen or fifteen years old my parents were told that in time, I would be lame due to a congenital deformity in both ankles. There was an experimental, corrective procedure available, if we were ready to consider it. The operations had to be performed before I was "fully grown". I had simultaneous surgeries on both legs. I was told that the operations lasted six hours. The senior surgeon was Dr. Genestras, a renowned orthopedist. Post operatively, I spent six months in a rehabilitation facility in White Plains. I think it was the forerunner of Burke Institute. Heavy plaster casts covered the full length of both legs. As I was healing, when the weather was warm, my legs itched "like crazy", under the plaster casts. I found relief by scratching them with a long knitting needle.

The food in the rehab facility was not kosher. I tried to accommodate my dietary restrictions. Sunday mornings was a treat for the patients. They gave each patient a portion of bacon. I would hold up the bacon, swaying it back and forth and selectively portion or auction it off. I was quite popular, certainly on Sunday mornings! No children were allowed to visit the residents of the rehab facility. My parents came every Sunday. I missed my sisters and could only see them through the window.

I had missed a full term in High School. When discharged, I was advised that I had no restrictions except "thou shall not ski". I could never break an ankle, I could only shatter it. I guess since I had leg surgeries and limitations I've not ever been athletic. In a way I've sort of been a "klutz".

When I returned home, my parents hired a tutor for me, in order to make up the time I missed in high school. They hired Herbert Dean, a brilliant high school student. He was tall, thin with an enormous Adam's apple. For a year I had a crush on him. He was an excellent tutor. I completed the semester in a very short time, took the required state regents, achieved high grades in each and thus was able to graduate on time. The next term I also resumed my activities in a number of extra-curricular clubs. I remember that my father designed and manufactured sterling silver pins for the French club, a fleur de lis, and for Natura, the biology club, a spider web. I volunteered in the Latin Department. The office was on the second floor of an old wooden structure. It was the original building that housed Erasmus Hall Academy, built in 1786. The building has since achieved landmark status. Dr Wedeck, a classics scholar, was the Department Head. I studied Latin. I don't remember much except "amo, amas, amat". Studying Latin has helped me over the years to decipher the meaning of words in English. Dr. Wedeck was a gifted mentor who even tried to teach me Greek. I never got beyond it, it all remained "Greek to me".

High school memories are somewhat limited and disjointed. I attended when Europe, not the U.S., was already embroiled in the throes of World War II. One afternoon, a classmate invited me to a newly formed, after-school club. He said that I would be an ideal member. The boys all wore dark brown shirts. As I sat there, I became increasingly uncomfortable. It was my first exposure to a pro Nazi, anti-Semitic group and I was at a loss of how to respond. I ended up running out of the meeting, later mentally kicking myself for not objecting vocally to the group. Instead, I took the coward's way out. This was in 1937, when we were not yet fully aware of what really was going on in Europe.

Obviously, seeds of hate were already being sown, even in the U.S.

I was enrolled in a French honor class. The day Paris fell in the Spring of 1940, Monsieur Hemon, our wonderful French teacher, stood in front of the class. He told us, with tears flowing down his cheeks, of the tragic event that Paris had fallen. We all stood up and spontaneously began to sing La Marseillaise. It's a high school memory I will never forget.

I attended Hebrew High School and Erasmus Hall High School concurrently. Hebrew classes were held three evenings a week and Sundays at the Yeshivah of Flatbush. Only a handful of students participated in what was, presumably, an experimental Hebrew high school program. Not many students chose to extend their Hebrew education after a full day of classes in public high school. I graduated from the program and continued my Hebrew education at Hertzeliah Hebrew Academy. Classes were held in the old Forwards building on East Broadway, in downtown Manhattan. That meant that I had to travel by subway after school to Hebrew classes. By that time I was already enrolled in Brooklyn College. Once again I'm getting ahead of chronology.

FRIEDA

My mother went to the hospital for an "exploratory operation", a suspected tumor on her adrenal gland. She must have had a premonition of her dire diagnosis. She left notes of instruction all over the house, from the schedule for watering the plants, to leaving payment for the milkman in the glass milk bottle that was in an insulated container outside our front door, to helping Ronnie get ready for bed and not forgetting to kiss her.

I vividly recall and re-live the last time I sat at my mother's bedside. Her coal-black, wavy hair framing her face. She looked very serious and said that she had something very important to ask of me. She held my hand and periodically gently curved her hand over my head and cheeks. "Devorahlah, as you grow up, you will learn that there are two things no one can ever take away from you, maintaining a good name and your education. Earn them both and you will always have and keep them. I would like you to promise me that you will see to it that you and your sisters will each graduate from college. Will you promise me that?" I said "of course" and snuggled next to her in bed, feeling her warmth, not her pain. She hugged and kissed me as she caressed my head. It was the last time I was with and cuddled by my loving mother. She died a few days later, on May 17, 1939. She was 36 years young.

I recall a quotation from Rabbi Shaul Praver, who said, "The secret of Jewish survival is to meet tragedy with resolve and thrive." I realize somehow, that even a tragic, traumatic event in life opened the door and enabled a positive aspect to enter. If my mother had not died so young, I don't think that her values, her example, the role model she was for me, would have become my guiding compass. Although I have never achieved in my nineties, what my mother was at thirty six, she has been my "GPS", my "Gracious Personal Sage".

My mother, as young as she was, was a matriarch of not only our nuclear family, but her extended family as well. She instilled in us a legacy of guidelines to try to follow, including love of family, pride in and appreciation of our heritage, Judaism, care for those in need, focus on education and achieving and sustaining a good name. She not only spoke of these values, they were also evidenced by her actions.

My father was left with three daughters. I was 16, my sister Evelyn was 13, my little sister Ronya was just six years old and my grieving father was 43. It was quite a challenge. He was busy arranging for the funeral and asked me to pick up the death certificate from the hospital. I wanted to pick up my mommy and bring her home, not a piece of paper! I went to the appropriate office in the hospital. I sat on a hard bench outside the office and waited and waited...I was 16 years old, sad and scared. It seemed like an interminable wait. Two young doctors were near me. I assumed they were doctors since they were in white coats and had stethoscopes dangling around their necks. One said to the other, "What the hell are we to put down?". On the death certificate, I was later told, the recorded "cause of death" was the technical term for her heart stopped beating! My father was informed that gangrene had set in and there was negligence on the part of the hospital. He was advised to sue the hospital. To which he responded, "There is no point in suing. It won't bring back the mother of my children nor my Frieda. I'm not a litigious person."

Ronya, age 6 and My Father
Jones Beach, 1939

It was decided that Ronya would not go to the funeral. However, someone had to tell her that Mommy died. I was given the unhappy assignment by my Dad. I tried to explain the unfathomable, with the flawed sensitivity of a 16 year old teenager. I told my six year old baby sister that God chose special people as angels. He needed a special angel and Mommy was chosen. To this day I can see her tear filled eyes and her little, poignant, somber face. As her anger welled up, she slapped my face and shouted "But I need her too!". No, the slap didn't hurt me. Her pain, her loss, her vulnerability – that remains in my heart and mind.

When it came time to set up a grave stone we chose one carved with a budding tree. Mommy loved plants and flowers. She was especially fond of lilacs. We wanted something special engraved on the stone to represent her unfinished life. Mar Rabinowitz helped to compose a Hebrew poem for us. It was characteristic of the support and the special relationship we had with some of our elementary school teachers in the yeshivah.

ACCOMMODATIONS
AND ADJUSTMENTS

The period that followed Mommy's death is fogged by time and interspaced with a contaminated memory. Unfortunately I don't have anyone to either refresh memories, or validate facts. Be that as it may, I recall that we had a series of hired "homemakers". One was a German woman , with a heavy accent, who ordered us around like a Gestapo officer. She didn't last too long. We finally worked out our "Berlinger modus operandi". Each of us had certain responsibilities. Daddy did most of the shopping on Sundays and prepared some food as well, for the upcoming week. Daddy came home with recipes and ended up being a pretty good cook, but with a relatively limited repertoire. He did make great blintzes. A favorite frequent supper was broiled minute steak, a baked potato and string beans, which I recall having several times a week.

Sometime during this period we got a hybrid Spitz and "something" poodle. Evie and Ronnie were enthralled with the dog, "Buddy". They even slept with the dog at their feet. I did not. When they grew up and away, they each owned a dog or a cat. So do my children. I never wanted one. I can only attribute it possibly to the experience I had when

Buddy died. The dog, on hot dog days in the summer, would lie on the tile bathroom floor next to the tub. There was no air conditioning in those days. Buddy probably found the coolest spot in the house. When he died in the bathroom, presumably of old age, no one wanted to handle him. I was given the job to carry his stiff corpse out of the house and dispose of him. It was a very unpleasant experience.

Ronya and Buddy   *Evelyn and Buddy*
On East 5th Street, Brooklyn

FRIENDS

Daddy always encouraged having our home as the center of our social life. Our friends always congregated there. Daddy was a favorite among them. In retrospect, I realize that he was able to graciously monitor the activities and friends of his two teen age daughters. He also enjoyed the company of our generation. During the late 1930's and early 1940's we socialized primarily in groups. There seemed to be much less individual coupling. Even when we did couple, we went in groups. Living in Brooklyn, none of us had a car. Public transportation was readily available. As we got older, if the group ever went out of town, e.g. for a picnic, we arranged to hire a bus and driver. At the time, neither drugs nor alcohol were problems. I don't think they were problems not only in our group, but not a major factor generally in our generation. It was a good time for growing up.

My two closest friends were Meechal Hendel, later Steinmetz and Selma Levine, later Zorn. I met each one in my teens and our friendships continued way into adulthood. As I write this and think of both of them, I realize that they were as different as two individuals could be. They did not know one another, but knew of each other. How were they different? Let me count the ways:

Meechal was an observant, Orthodox Jew. She was a practical individual, unsophisticated, down to earth in her approach. She was not interested in art, literature or politics. She was steeped in the Jewish religion and culture. She was honest, caring, generous and outgoing. She loved Israeli dancing. We met in a Zionist youth group. I was initially impressed by her skill and enthusiasm with dancing. In later years, when we were both engaged, we always double dated. Our husbands became close friends as well. She and her husband, Jack, had four daughters, Debby, Esther, Barbara (now Bryna) and Deena. As their daughters grew and married young, they chose increasingly more religious, observant spouses. Meechal became more observant in her religious practices as well. For example, she had her hair covered at all times. She never wasted time; she was frequently either praying or knitting lovely items for her growing family. Their daughters gave them 49 grandchildren! I remember advice Meechal gave me when I asked her about handling the prospect of being a grandparent: "Debbie", she said, "zip your mouth and unzip your purse." Each of her daughters ran a lovely home and family. Today their immediate family has grown into a dynasty. In our teenage years Meechal and I confided in each other for hours on the phone about our perspectives on life, our dates and social life. When we were older, advice revolved about child rearing and homemaking. Meechal was an *Ayshet Chayal*, the Hebrew expression for a "woman of valor", and indeed she was.

Selma on the other hand, was a secular Jew. We met, as I mentioned, at the bus stop on our way to high school. Early on, we were so close and fond of each other that my father designed and made a gold ring for her birthday. Selma was politically astute. Her orientation was very liberal. She was a creative, talented, very bright individual. Whatever hobby, medium or material she chose, she excelled in it. Be it pottery, paint, clay, sculpting, calligraphy, sewing clothes for her children or the dolls in dioramas. She fashioned things of beauty. She did not attend college, even though she was brighter than most of our peers. She had a mordant sense of humor. Additionally, she was a caring and generous individual. She and her husband Bruce had two children, Francine and Jonathan. Both were adorable and loving. When it came to the children and later grandchildren, Selma was a worry bug. We confided in each other, psychologically supported each other, and when the need was there, she was there. I felt as close to Selma as I did to my sisters. We remained close well into our seventies and then she drifted away. Despite efforts on my part and members of both families, we never found out what precipitated the change in her feeling toward and for me. I was pained. Somewhere in my myriad files is a poem or paragraph I wrote at the time, entitled "Elegy for a Dead Friendship". In recent years we did reconnect, but never on the level of prior times.

So, there is the picture of both women; each one different from the other in multiple ways. Yet both of them touched my heart and remain there. Both of them have since passed away. I miss each one and the gift they bestowed on me by being there.

SUMMER CAMP

Ronnie went to Cejwin, a sleep away camp, for several summers. I was a counselor there one summer, where and when I met Shirley Liebowitz, later Horowitz. We were counselors in buddy bunks and have retained our friendship to this day. A number of years ago we traveled together with our spouses as a foursome. Today, as a senior, Shirley continues to seek and carry out ventures on her "bucket list". So far she has, to name a few, ridden on a motorcycle, gone wind surfing, jumped from a plane in a parachute and taken a ride in a hot air balloon! No telling what self- challenges Shirley will meet next. She is a prolific reader, avid traveler and a delight to be with.

During the summer, when Ronnie was a camper and I was a counselor in Cejwin, my father married Dora, a woman much younger, who had been his secretary for several years. She was heavy set, heavily made up and heavily perfumed. I disliked her when I first met her and liked her even less after she married my father. In retrospect it was mutual. I found her to be manipulative and self-centered. From my perspective, at no point in her marriage did she give my Dad's welfare priority, despite his illness. They were married some time after his first heart attack. Be it diet or activities, she did not abide by, or consider his physical or medical limitations. It was that aspect of her behavior that bothered me the most and that I resented. I shared my concern with her and was advised "to mind your own business". Evie and Ronnie ostensibly had a slightly more positive relationship with Dora. Dora and I continued to have a mutual dislike and distrust of each other for many years, even after my father died. Although my father was undoubtedly aware of our relationship, we never discussed or alluded to it. Part of his modus operandi was to passively leave unpleasant aspects alone.

In order to attend Brooklyn College one had to apply and pass a qualifying exam. I was delighted to attend. I could even walk to school! When my cousin Ruth was living with us she had suggested that I major in nutrition. It was presumably a "safe" field. During the Depression that meant that you could find a job when you graduated. I also minored in education so that I would be qualified to teach home economics. Had I explored my real interests, I probably would have veered in another direction. Medicine, psychiatry and psychology all seemed appealing. However, growing up during the Depression, the impact of the economy guided my ultimate choice. The nutrition curriculum included a number of science courses. I was accustomed to being a good student and achieving good grades. I worked for them. When I flunked the first and only course in my life, I was devastated! That thwarted my plans to possibly major in science. It was the first course in chemistry. The professor failed a good number of other students in the class as well. I don't recall grades I achieved in the rest of my 121 credits in college, but I'll never forget that "F" in chemistry by Professor Concklin. Incidentally, his name is also the only faculty name I recall.

Writing about negative school memories, an experience from elementary school comes back to mind. We had so few students in the Yeshivah of Flatbush at that time, the teaching staff had to recruit students from lower grades to participate in the graduation play. The operetta, the Mikado, was to be presented. There weren't enough students in the class to be a chorus. When the music teacher auditioned me and my classmate, Hortense Rosen, we were both told we would be in the chorus, but we were to only "mouth" the songs and not vocalize. I can hear his instructions to this day. The only comforting aspect of the experience was that I was not alone. My dear friend, Horty, and I were a silent duet.

Sometime during my first or second year in college, following up on my activities in Zionist organizations, I thought I might like to emigrate to Israel as a *chalutzah* (a pioneer). That involved a certain degree of pre-preparation. So, for a short period, every weekend, with a male friend, we thumbed rides from Brooklyn, N.Y. to Hightstown, N.J. It was a far safer time to hitchhike. There was a commune of young people in Hightstown who were training to go and work on a *kibbutz* (collective) in Israel. They welcomed our interest, participation and labor. I was initially assigned to harvesting potatoes. There were limited sleeping quarters for weekend "guests" or more accurately "labor". The girls slept on straw mats in a section of the chicken house. Yes, chicken house! The chickens were there too! I don't know where the guys slept, but I'm sure it was equally accommodating. It seemed like a great deal, only when you are young.

THE WAR YEARS AND BEYOND

When I first started college we were not yet at war; England was. Our participation in the conflict was peripheral. Khaki colored wool was distributed to volunteers and we knitted scarves for the British soldiers. The project was called "Knitten for Britain". The arrangement was, if you were knitting during class, the instructor could not ask you to stop. It was a great activity during boring lectures.

Although the United States had not yet declared war, the R.O.T.C. (Reserved Officers Training Corps) were on many campuses. Many citizens and students felt that the reason to enter the war raging in Europe, was justifiable. Hence the objection to R.O.T.C. on college campuses was limited. It was very different during subsequent unpopular wars. Brooklyn College had a R.O.T.C. unit on campus. On warm days, with windows wide open, the cadence of their marching boots and voices wafted into the lecture halls, often competing with the lecturer. In view of the draft and the lottery, it was great to have so many young men on campus!

I will always recall standing on the quadrangle, listening to President Roosevelt on the loudspeaker declaring war. I looked around at some of the male students, friends, and wondered how many of them may not return from the war. I vividly remember the face of one of my friends who never did return. I get goose pimples when I think and write about my backward glance and his face, chalked on the slate of my memory.

Although we were at war and there was a paucity of young men, I had an active social life, dating friends who had deferments. We had a cohesive group of young adults who were involved in protesting the Nazi onslaught. We marched, wrote letters to President Roosevelt, attended a massive protest rally in Madison Square Garden and were actively involved with Zionist organizations.

At the same time that I was studying at Brooklyn College, I was continuing my Hebrew studies. I transferred from Herziliah which was located downtown in the Forwards building, to the Jewish Theological Seminary at Broadway and West 122nd Street. It was a *shlepp* (drag)! I had decided to pursue a BHL degree concurrently with the BA from Brooklyn College. I did not transfer any of my college credits for either the BHL or BA degrees. Between the Brooklyn College courses and those at the Seminary, I was carrying the equivalent of about 33 college credits each semester. Classes at the Seminary were three nights a week and Sundays. After 9 P.M., when the weekday Seminary classes were over, I walked, frequently alone, from the

Seminary across Morningside Park to the 125th St. subway stop on the D train of the Independent subway line. I rode to the last stop, Church Avenue in Brooklyn. I imagine, no way, would one currently take that walk through the park at night. When I reached home, sometime around 11 P.M., after a half hour walk from Church avenue, I did my homework for my college courses. It was a busy time.

Toward the end of my last semester at Brooklyn College, I had to do student teaching in my major, home economics. I was assigned to James Madison High School. It was in an upper middle class neighborhood, not too far from the college. One of the last days of the term, the supervising teacher said she was leaving the classroom and that I should oversee the end of the session, which involved cleanup. I followed the standard procedure and assigned the routine chore to one of the students. The student lifted a large sharp knife, came behind me, placed the knife at my back, cut through my blouse and punctured my bra. The tip of the knife did not pierce my skin. She had moved the knife very slowly, not thrusting it into my back, but I could feel the tip of the knife against my skin. She was much taller than me. She leaned down and said in a menacing tone into my ear, "whose gonna clean up?" I replied that I would take over. She pulled the knife back, dropped it and ran out. The other students, all girls, scooted out of the room. No one intervened. I was shaken. That incident presented a dilemma as well as a decision. Should I press charges? If so, there would be consequences for the teacher and the student. It was during the last week of the semester. I decided not to press charges. I did give the teacher a full verbal report. I was not injured, only my blouse. The student had carved more than my blouse. That incident, as well as my student teaching experience, carved my vocational future. I realized that in New York City high schools, home economics was assigned to marginal pupils, those with academic and or behavioral problems. I did not want to teach home economics on the secondary level.

EVENTFUL ENGAGEMENT

I had a full, lively social life with many friends and I was also involved in a number of clubs and organizations. In my senior year in college, I was engaged to Jerome Robbins. We had attended elementary school together and were friends intermittently for many years. I dated a number of "young men", as the saying goes, during high school and in college. Toward the end of my college days, and nights, Jerry and I reconnected and fell in love. It was a breathtaking, glorious courtship. We had so much in common. As a youngster, Jerry was the "shortest, fastest and smartest kid" in the class. He matured into a relatively tall, handsome, bright, talented, perceptive young man with a wonderful sense of humor and zest for life. I remember he had developed hypnosis as a skill. He was able to hypnotize several subjects in a group and then bring them "out of it". We never realized, at that time, that there was a potential danger in hypnotizing subjects, not knowing anything about them. He did it to entertain. No, I was not hypnotized by him; I was well aware of why I loved him. We hoped that our mutual history was a prelude to a loving future. I was so happy.

I loved his mother Taube as well. She was a

bright, loving individual. Apparently I was also missing "mother love". My relationship with his father and younger brother, Bobby, was great.

Jerome (Jerry) Robbins and His parents
Taube and Saul. Fall, 1944

I recall one lovely, sunny afternoon Jerry and I spent in Central Park. We were lying on the grass, I was in his arms with my head on his chest. My ear was pressed against the fabric of his shirt and I was listening to the syncopated thumping of his heart. I felt an overwhelming sense of a life force. It was an unforgettable moment etched in memory.

At the time there was a national draft. Jerry had a legitimate exemption. He was attending Yeshivah University, a senior, majoring in literature. He planned to be a writer. We were both 20 years old.

Jerry purchased a beautiful diamond engagement ring designed and made by my father, at a good price I am sure. My skilled father fashioned things of beauty. He also made a 14 k gold, Brooklyn College class ring which I gave Jerry as an engagement gift.

I graduated from Brooklyn College in June 1944 and started job hunting immediately during the summer for a position in the commercial realm. I applied for a job at the National Safety Bank & Trust Co., near my father's office. The training period initially involved working on the floor above the street level, copying and tallying numbers. Boring. Aside from the lack of intellectual stimulation there was also a paucity of chairs. Yes, chairs. There just weren't enough chairs for the number of employees. They were missing about three. No working stations or chairs were assigned. It was first come, first sit. It depended when one arrived in the morning and when one returned from lunch. It was a crazy situation. I lasted one week and resigned. I literally could not stand that job.

I next decided that I would try to find a position related to home economics, once again in the commercial realm. I couldn't find any. So I decided I would even apply for a position as a hostess in the Child's restaurant chain. I filled out the application. Then, before I was even interviewed, the personnel director, looked at my application, then at me, directly in the eye, and said : "I'm sorry, but we do not employ persons of your persuasion". I was devastated! It was my first experience of being discriminated against for being Jewish. I had grown up cocooned in primarily a Jewish world. Today it would never happen. What did I do? I was so upset, I went to my father's office, two blocks away and "cried my eyes out"! So much for my venture into the alien, commercial world.

Jerry enlisted in the U.S. Army, despite his exemption. He felt very strongly that he had to fight Hitler and to try to "right the wrong". Shortly before he left for the service he wrote a poem entitled "Wait For Me World". The poem was published in 1944 before he left, as an end paper in the Sunday magazine edition of *PM*.

WAIT FOR ME WORLD

Wait for me, World.
I have a rendezvous
far, far away.
It won't be play;
rather, shall we say,
business.

Where - I know not, nor do I know
whom I shall meet.
Yet this I know -
I must go.

I don't want to leave -

no one ever does;
yet there are times when one does
not what one wants,
but what one must.

So I must leave.

Before I go I exact a promise
from you.
The hope for its fulfillment
is all that sends me away now.

Promise to remain
the same
till my return.
No - not in all ways.
Change is part of Life.
In fact, I might say I leave now
because I desire some changes
and want to help
bring them about.

Yet these are the things
which I hope
will ever be the same
forever more ....

Promise me there will always be -
the sun and moon and stars
as signs of the Infinite;
exalting Man even as they
humble him.

Promise there will always be love;

The love of family,
whom I hurt momentarily
in order to bring them eventual
    security;
Then love of friends,
whose warm smiles mean so much
more than can be put on paper;
and last, because the closest at heart,
the love of one particular person -
a pure love, given freely,
completely, steadfastly
an intangible - like air -
which alone makes all tangibles meaningful.

Promise me there will be
music and laughter -
the free, unforced laughter of
untroubled minds,
who fear not the horrible visage of
the idiot Mars.

Promise me there will be
freedom -
Not the freedom to starve
without restraint,
nor the freedom to crush
another under the false guise
of "business" or "politics" -
but freedom from want
and from fear;
freedom to say and do as
one wishes, without hurting another.

These are the things for which I

will yearn -
have them ready for my return.

Remember, World - it is for
these I fight -
You must not fail me.
Once again - lest you forget -
Wait for me, World -
I will be back....
    Pvt. Jerome Robbins
                        1944

He clarified his motivation for enlisting and his
goals. Well, the world did not wait for him. He was
killed in action on December 25, 1944 at the age of
21.

DEVASTATING DILEMMAS

What do I recall from that period? Pain. Grief. I felt as if I was being hurled and tossed around. I thought that my life had been locked into a secure future and now I was catapulted into "nowhere to go or be".

Sustaining my own, I also felt a need to be supportive of his family. I spent much time with them. Most memories of that mourning and adjusting period are veiled and curtained away in forgotten memories. But I do vividly recall two events.

One was the last time I saw Jerry, when he came home on leave, just before he was sent overseas. His family lived in the Washington Heights area of Manhattan, a long subway ride from Brooklyn. When I was ready, reluctantly, to go home, Jerry walked me to the subway station. We kissed good-bye on the station plaza. I recall as we kissed, I had an overwhelming feeling of tragedy engulfing me. Did it portend the catastrophe that was about to befall us in a few months? When I sat down in the train I began uncontrollable sobbing. The train had few passengers. A woman came up to me to offer help. I cried "all the way home".

The second event I recall was when I was at his

parents' apartment. I had already known that he had been killed. I was handed the confirmation. A pale yellow thin sheet of paper, the telegram. The tragic news printed on strips, pasted on yellow paper, the letters in caps clawing my eyes, the words piercing my heart: "WE REGRET TO INFORM YOU...."

At the time, I finally had a position as a teacher in an elementary school, in an orthodox yeshivah, the Yeshivah of Brighton Beach and Vicinity. I was hired by the principal of the school's secular studies, a friend, Rabbi Albert Lewis, to teach the seventh grade. I also referred Shirley Flam for a teaching position in the school. Shirley and I were friends as pupils in the Yeshivah of Flatbush. She was hired and now we were in school together again.

When Jerry was killed my world and plans were turned upside down. "Me" had nowhere to be or go. It was, in a way, a similar scenario flashing back to when my mother died. Although my family, friends and colleagues were incredibly supportive, I felt that I had to make some definitive changes. I had to get away.

The reality of making a change jarred me back to the bedside promise I made to my mother. Education was the venue to the end goal, a degree, not only for me but for my sisters as well. I still had another year to complete my degree at the Seminary. So, I decided to complete it, finish my teaching commitment and postpone "getting away". So I did.

DEDICATION TO DAUNTING
DIPLOMAS

I spent the next few months exploring, surveying and assessing the next steps. I realized after a term's experience teaching in elementary school that I preferred dealing with children one at a time, not as a group. I was also motivated to work with their parents. Those realizations convinced me to change my vocational plans. I looked into an emerging field, guidance and counseling. Research led me to a program in Ohio at Western Reserve University (today, Case Western Reserve). It was an experimental offering, starting for the first time in the Fall, at the Graduate School, with courses also to be taken in the School of Social Work and the Medical School. The year long program led to a Masters degree in guidance and counseling. It looked to be an answer to my quest. I applied and was accepted along with two other students; a small experimental program indeed.

Classes in Cleveland started in the Fall. I was teaching and still attending the Jewish Theological Seminary, working toward a BHL degree. I had another year to complete the degree. How could I leave? I hit on a plan. I applied and convinced the administration of the Seminary to be granted permission to complete my last year with independent study. If I took and passed all the exams, I would be granted the degree and graduate a year earlier. It worked. I don't know how I did it. That June I took and passed, I think it was fifteen, sixteen or more final examinations, the equivalent of four semesters! And so I participated in the 1945, instead of the 1946, graduation exercises held on the beautiful Jewish Theological Seminary quadrangle. I was awarded my coveted BHL degree. My mental message to my mom was "I did it because of you Mommy".

My friend and colleague, Shirley Flam, wanted to make a change as well. She applied and was also accepted to the Graduate School at Western Reserve, with a major in English literature. Thereafter we made our explorations together.

First on the list was housing. We found a studio apartment in a residential hotel within walking distance of University Circle. The apartment was on the ground floor of the Doanbrook Hotel. It was just opposite the concierge hotel desk. The staff adopted us and screened every male visitor! Our apartment consisted of a large furnished living room with a murphy (pull down) bed, a full bathroom and a kitchen alcove. I can just imagine what Shirley and I would be classified as today! (No, we weren't and aren't.)

Next, I felt that I should try to support myself

and so I applied for a teaching job at the Bureau of Jewish Education. It was serendipity in that I met Fran Turner, the secretary of the Bureau. She expedited and executed the successful running of the Bureau, as well as easing our adjustment to Cleveland. I arrived in Cleveland a short time before the semester began and settled in. I became acquainted with the Hebrew school curriculum and schedule. It involved teaching Hebrew grammar, history and literature several late afternoons and Sunday mornings.

Once Shirley arrived, we set up semi-housekeeping. Since both Shirley and I observed *kashrut* (Jewish dietary laws), we found it easier to accommodate our mutual needs. Fran was most helpful in referring us to resources. The kosher butcher was delighted with two young, new customers. At that time the koshering (soaking and salting the meat according to Jewish dietary laws) was done by the customers in their own homes, not by butchers or the commercial providers, as it is today. Chickens were never sold in parts. Yet, Shirley and Deborah could order half a chicken and our butcher gladly koshered it for us. He would even kosher a chicken liver by broiling it and send it along with our order. I do not think he had any customers who ordered less and received so much service gratis!

We walked to classes. I was even able to walk to

the Bureau for teaching assignments. The Bureau was at the edge of Wade Park. The views of the park and the lake enhanced my teaching experience.

We had arrived in Cleveland a few weeks before the holiday of Rosh Hashanah. Fran graciously invited us for the holiday meals to her home. We became friendly with her family. Our warm relationship with them continued for many years. We were able to attend synagogue holiday services literally "down the block". The beautiful Temple presided by Rabbi Abba Hillel Silver was only a block away. We heard many inspiring sermons enhanced by his "silvery" voice. We also took advantage of the city's and university's cultural offerings. One of the highlights was hearing concerts at Severance Hall conducted by George Szell and then taking a short walk back to our abode.

While we were at Western Reserve I met Marcia Silverstein, later Sheiman. I don't remember where or when. The unifying element was that we were both from Brooklyn and Jewish. Our friendship has lovingly flourished to this day. Marcia was in the School of Social Work and I think we may have had some classes together as well.

My student placement, as part of the degree requirement, involved an internship at the Jewish Vocational Service, located in downtown Cleveland. It was an excellent experience. My supervisor and colleagues trained me so that by the end of the program, I felt ready to assume the role and responsibilities of a vocational counselor. They even offered me a position upon graduation. That was not an option for me. I had to get back home. My year away was over.

For a long time I had a yen to take an "aeroplane ride". That is what we called it in the 30's and 40's. So, after graduation and arrangements were made to move back to Brooklyn, I purchased a one way ticket to Idlewild Airport N.Y., now Kennedy. When I arrived, I called my father to let him know that I was back from Cleveland. When he asked where I was, so he could pick me up, I told him "at the airport". I understand that he blanched and almost fainted. It was unusual for the average traveler to go by plane for a short flight, at that time. We didn't know anyone personally who flew. I was thrilled. To this day, I still am at the prospect of a flight.

Retracing the events and experiences of my life is at times enjoyable. At other times I have difficulty recalling, or even accessing words. Memories can be contaminated by time and one's mental capacities. I think of memories as being stored in the library of the brain where one can borrow or return them. Another way is to think of memories as accumulating in a bank, where one deposits new memories or accesses older ones as withdrawals, some to be re-deposited in the same or different form. At other times, accounts are closed. As I write and I reach a blank, I realize that I tend to focus on process rather than content. I'm not sure whether I am writing an autobiography or a memoir. Whatever it is, it's slow going. I probably will continue to intersperse the events with comments of this nature.

PERFECT PREMIER
PROFESSIONAL POSITION

After I returned home from Cleveland I found a
position as an assistant to the director of personnel
at the Jewish Child Care Association (JCCA). I loved
the work, the colleagues and the location. The
Jewish Federation building, in which we were
housed, was on west 47th street between 5th and 6th
avenues in Manhattan, directly across the street
from my father's office! Whenever he wanted to see
me, he would put a placard in the window.

My boss, Lucille Lazar, was a wonderful mentor
and role model. She was the Director of Personnel.
She was totally deaf, yet skilled in many ways
despite the handicap. She was able to participate
actively in labor negotiations, representing the
administration of JCCA, with a very large liberal
labor union on the other side. Frequently the
negotiations went into the wee hours of the night
and she continued with wit and vigor. Since she was
deaf I would write down a summary of the points
made by the labor negotiator and she responded
verbally. She had taken elocution lessons over the
years and was fantastic in her verbal responses.
Many of the deliberate distractions and evasions
were eliminated and she was able to cut through to

the essence of the current issue. She frequently attributed her success to my notes. My additional responsibilities on the job included hiring and firing personnel, participating in composing and editing the personnel manual, as well as serving as Lucille's recording ears and being a member of the negotiating team. I loved working with her.

Another colleague who enhanced my "job satisfaction index" was Lillian (Lilly) Turitz, Lucille's assistant. I learned much from both women and I attribute a portion of my professional ongoing development to their influence.

LOVE, LIBERTY AND MY PURSUIT OF HAPPINESS

Irving Eiferman and I corresponded during the war. In our early twenties, we had both been co-presidents of Masada, a Zionist youth group. In prior years we dated other partners, never each other. The salutation in his letters from overseas was frequently *lehitraot*, which means "be seein' you". We had been platonic friends for a number of years prior to the war. Irving wrote to me when I was studying in Cleveland that he was recently discharged from service and has returned to school. He was completing his law degree which was interrupted when he went into the service.

Irving in service. Drawing by Carl Paul Jennewein, famous artist and sculptor (e.g. works in Rockefeller Center, Philadelphia Museum of Art).

Irv began to write with increasing frequency. Our correspondence not only became more frequent but also more affectionate. When I returned from Cleveland in the late Spring of 1946, his visits, in lieu of letters, were frequent as our relationship intensified and blossomed. We had an exciting new relationship. We were in love! Each of us was busy all day, he in school and I working at JCCA. Almost every evening Irv would take the Coney Island avenue trolley car to my home on East 5th street and then back home in the wee hours of the morning. I don't know when he got his homework done, because the trolley schedule was limited at night. I had always admired his mind and his ability in public speaking. Other aspects of Irving "got to me". Apparently, thanks to the infrequent schedule of the trolley and the nudging of his father, he finally consulted with my dad. A beautiful diamond engagement ring was designed and crafted. Irv proposed in his parents kitchen on March 8, 1947, his birthday. My acceptance was a "foregone" conclusion. Our plans were to be married after he graduated and passed the bar exam.

In the meantime my sister Evie graduated from City College with a major in accounting. She was dating David Wagner steadily. It was an exciting time in our family. Evie and David were engaged shortly after Irving and me. They planned to get married about a few weeks before us. My father said "NO". He wasn't about to plan, host and invite some of the same people to two weddings, weeks apart. So, Irv and I moved up our date and Evie and David postponed their date. We all compromised and agreed on December 13, 1947. It would be a double wedding!

Double Engagement

Mr. and Mrs. Jack Berlinger of 777 E. 5th St. announce the double engagement of their daughters, Miss Deborah Berlinger, to Irving Eiferman, son of Mr. and Mrs. Eiferman of Brooklyn, and Miss Evelyn Berlinger, to David Wagner, son of Mr. and Mrs. Abraham Wagner, also of Brooklyn.

The brides-elect attended the Yeshiva of Flatbush and graduated from Brooklyn College and the College of the City of New York.

Mr. Eiferman is a senior at St. John's Law School. During the war he served with the U. S. Army throughout the China-Burma-India theater of operations. Mr. Wagner, an alumnus of the New School of Social Research, is now secretary-treasurer of the Indi Society of America. During th war he served with the 4th Ma rine Division in the Pacific.

The double wedding will be hel on Dec. 13 at the Aperion Mano

Engagement Announcement   *"We were engaged last night"*
1947, New York Times?   *March 9, 1947*

THE WEDDING

A mere 535 guests were invited! We had to accommodate seven families: David's mother and father's, Irving's mother and father's, Dora's family, our mother's family and our father's family plus our friends and acquaintances. My dad "went all out" in planning an elaborate affair. He loved entertaining and this was "right up his alley". Dora participated as well. Evie and I were tangential planners. It was exciting, stressful and busy, all at the same time.

In order to observe *halachic* (according to Jewish law) customs and requirements, we had two separate marriage ceremonies with the oldest daughter married first. Two different Rabbis conducted the ceremonies. Evie and David had David's Rabbi and we had Rabbi Harry Halperin whom I knew and greatly admired. Rabbi Halperin said that his wedding gift to us was conducting the marriage ceremony. I was very touched by this gesture. My father crafted gold cuff links as a "thank you" to him. We wanted the weddings to take place in Brooklyn. There was a limited selection of places that could accommodate "our crowd". We finally settled on the Aperion, a catering hall on Kings Highway. The one disadvantage, from my perspective, was that the bride had to emerge from the bride's room, and descend a tremendous flight of stairs as part of the wedding procession, as all eyes were upon her. I was petrified. Evie and I jointly chose our bridesmaids. We had a total of 15 from among our close friends and relatives. David and Irving selected 15 ushers. There was no color scheme for the bridesmaids. Ronya, our "baby sister" was the maid of honor for both of us. Irv chose his friend, Sidney Fisher, as his best man. There was only one procession of the attendants, but two separate ceremonies. My father hired a well known Cantor to sing. I think his name was Shicoff.

With trepidation, I s-l-o-w-l-y went down the steps and down the aisle. My father and Dora met me at the foot of the stairs to accompany me the rest of the way. I remember thinking, "Mommy, you should be guiding my elbow, not her. I love and miss you." I don't remember any thing else about the ceremony except the one vital moment in my life, which to this day, almost 67 years later, is crystal clear in my mind and heart. Rabbi Halperin gestured to us to face one another. Sidney gave Irv the ring. Irv, pale with a serious expression on his face, repeated after Rabbi Halperin, *"Haray aht mehkudeshet lee"* ... "You are consecrated unto me".... It was at that moment that all the glitz and glamour faded away and Irv's gaze pierced my heart and soul. It was one of my most holy moments. I felt like crying and singing for joy at the same time. I was no longer just "me", it was a transformative moment to "we". As I write this, so many decades later, my eyes tear and I get goose pimples. The expression on Irv's face is etched in my heart's memory.

My colleague at JCCA, Lilly Turitz, noted the exact time that we became "man and wife", 9:17 PM. Thereafter, we always noted that moment when we celebrated our anniversary, not only on December 13th each year, but also on *Shabbos* Channukah, the Saturday night of Channukah. Whenever we were wedding guests, we adopted the practice of noting and informing the couple the exact time they became man and wife. The couple is always grateful. Each guest, at our wedding, had a "take home" gift of a champagne glass with their own initial etched on it. Someone helped themselves to Irving's and my glass. We were so disappointed about it that my father arranged to get a replacement for us. For years after, guests would show us the champagne glass they had kept as a souvenir of our wedding.

Evie and David's ceremony followed ours. I enjoyed their joining with a semi-maternal feeling. My sister Evie was a married woman and I now had a brother-in-law! It was quite an affair. There was even mention of "the double wedding of two sisters" in the New York Times.

Double Wedding for Sisters

Miss Deborah Berlinger and Miss Evelyn Berlinger, daughters of Mr. and Mrs. Jack Berlinger, of 777 East Fifth Street, Brooklyn, will be brides at a double wedding the evening of Dec. 13, at the Aperion, 813 Kings Highway. Miss Deborah Berlinger will be married to Mr. Irving Eiferman, son of Mr. and Mrs. Joseph Eiferman, of Brooklyn. Miss Evelyn Berlinger will be the bride of Mr. David Wagner, son of Mr. and Mrs. Abraham Wagner. Rabbi Harry Halpern will officiate.

Prior to the wedding period, my sisters and I continued to live in our childhood home. My father and Dora lived in a one bedroom apartment on Ocean Parkway a few blocks away. My father came "home" frequently. He decided to have a major renovation done on the house on East 5th street. The plans were that he, Dora and Ronnie would live on the first floor and either Evie and David or Irving and I would live in the Ocean Parkway apartment. The other couple would occupy the second floor of the renovated house. Both couples wanted the Ocean Parkway apartment. It was perfect for newlyweds. How to decide? Choose! So a coin was tossed and Evie and David won the choice apartment and Irving and I were relegated to remain in my childhood home. But, it had yet to be renovated.

It really wasn't a renovation, it was a major gutting of the structure. Just as an example of the process and progress: The house had two stories and a basement level. I remember sitting on the toilet in the basement, holding an umbrella over my head because it was raining and two stories above there wasn't any roof overhead! Rooms were reconfigured. The old eat-in, windowed kitchen became a windowed galley kitchen. Every window was replaced. The bathrooms were completely gutted, tiled and modernized. In our apartment a large center room was redesigned from a series of hallways and became the dining room facing an entranceway. My father designed the configurations and contracted the alterations without consulting an architect. He enjoyed supervising the project. It was a creative, all consuming venture for him. It took months to complete. Irving and I had very little to do with the planning and selection of decorations.

We ended up having a large, modern, elaborate 3 bedroom apartment. All we had to do was furnish it.

Back to the night we were married. I had packed a suitcase to take on our honeymoon and a small overnight case to take to the Essex Hotel, where we had reservations to stay that night. Inadvertently, the overnight case was left at Irv's parents' home. So instead of taking off to the hotel after the wedding, Irv had to go home to his parents!

When we got there the atmosphere was like a house in mourning. His mother was practically in tears. Irv was an only child and his parents, especially his mother, felt that she had lost him again. It was bad enough when he went into the service, and then overseas. Here she was again losing him, but this time seemed more permanent. When we arrived they were so happy to see us. Irv's mother excitedly showed us where we could live in Irv's bedroom. They would fix it up. She would do my laundry and cook our meals if we would only live with them. It was so hard for her to accept the reality of Irv never coming home to stay again. It was also difficult for us to convince them that we were refusing their gracious offer. She extracted a promise from us that every Friday night, we would come for dinner. So we did most weeks for several years, until the children were born. We left for the Essex as reality sank in.

THE HONEYMOON

We arrived at the Essex by cab. As the doorman was removing my case from the trunk of the cab, the case opened and my nightclothes spilled out. With a gleam and a grin, the doorman slowly took each item that had fallen out, shook it and folded each one slowly. I was mortified. We finally got to our room. As I got into bed, Irv, having taken a shower, as recommended to him by a friend, came charging out of the bathroom and leaped onto the bed. The foot of bed broke with the force of his jump! We couldn't stop laughing. We were relegated to a 45 degree angle for the rest of the night! It was a slippery slope. When it came time to leave, Irv dropped our key at the desk, said the bed needed to be repaired and quickly scooted away.

Evie and David stayed at the Waldorf Astoria. We arranged to have breakfast, or rather brunch, together, the next mid-morning at the Longchamps restaurant. The Essex, Waldorf and Longchamps were all elegant places. They were expensive places which we would never have gone to – but this was an exceptional, special and memorable time for the four of us. After brunch we all took off for our separate honeymoons. Evie and David honeymooned in Washington, D.C. and Irv and I went to Miami, Florida, via rail. Remember, air travel was not that popular at the time. We had decided not to engage a sleeper compartment. We sat up all night. I had a great shoulder to lean on.

The view from the Cavalier hotel in Miami Beach was facing the Atlantic. It was in the area which I think is now called South Beach. Our friends from Brooklyn, Adele and Irv Kelton, were living in Miami at the time and so we had the opportunity to get together.

We went one evening to a Hi-Li game. Just as a lark, we bet on the number 9:17. Neither one of us had ever seen Hi-Li before, nor did we bet. But, bet we did and won! We figured out that we had won enough money to stay in Miami for an extra week! I was on vacation at the time. So, I contacted the office and asked for an extended week without pay. Irv was not working; he had graduated from law school and was waiting for the Bar exam results before going job hunting. So we had an additional glorious honeymoon week. During that week we found out that Irv had passed the Bar! That was the best news of all!

Deborah and Irving's Honeymoon, Miami Beach, 1947

Evie and David, coincidentally, had a similar experience in that sometime, during their honeymoon, they gambled and came home, back to New York, with more money than when they left!

A cousin who owned the Liebis hotel chain, gave both couples, as a wedding gift, a stay at half price at the Hudson Hotel on 42nd street for as long as needed. Since the East 5th street renovation was not ready yet, it was an ideal gift. Each couple had a studio suite. We had a full bathroom and a bedroom furnished with a bed, dresser and easy chair. The vestibule had a sink, a two burner stove and a small refrigerator. Evie and David were directly on the floor below us with a duplicate place. We did not have a freezer, but when the weather was freezing, Evie and I would put the food outside, on the wide concrete sill. We had many a dinner together. We even entertained there. I remember having a New Year's Eve birthday party, shortly after we returned from our honeymoons. Evie, David and some of our mutual friends were our guests celebrating in that tiny studio. The bed served as the sofa.

The hotel was a perfect setting, location and arrangement for us. The four of us worked in Manhattan. Yes, Irv got a job as a bone fide attorney at Schenley's distillery headquarters. I think they were located on 34th street. I worked on 47th street between 5th and 6th avenues. So, each morning we both walked to Broadway and 42nd street, kissed and Irv turned south and I went north to our places of employment. It was so great to walk to work. At night, after dinner, we frequently saw a Broadway show and walked back to the hotel when it was over. During that period we attended every play and show on Broadway! Tickets were reasonable in those days. Room service cleaned the studio and provided linens. What a life, and what a way to start a marriage! Evie and I shared much during that period as well as during the years that followed. David and Irv bonded as brothers. Since we lived at the hotel for six months it was an extended honeymoon for both couples.

FIRST APARTMENT

When the renovations were completed, we moved into a very elaborate apartment. It was so different that I didn't feel as if I was living in the house in which I grew up. When it came time to choose wall paper for our apartment, I stupidly didn't take time off from work, so I lived thereafter with very colorful walls. The elaborate wall paper patterns were duplicated in both apartments. Since then, my walls have always been painted white, beige or in pale tones without pattern. My father and Dora lived in the downstairs apartment with Ronya. I hardly remember anything about their apartment other than the bed was heart shaped and there were a number of mirrored walls.

My father gave each couple a bedroom set as a wedding gift. We did the shopping and choosing. We picked a lovely blond wood set from John Widdicomb and also some pieces from John Stuart. I love the set which has served me well to this day. It was fun furnishing our home. Irv and I had different tastes. Each item was chosen because we both liked it, not a concession to the other. That seemed to set the modus operandi for our future. I think, that as the years went on, we had a melding of not only our taste but our approach to many matters.

For example, when we were first married, as was the custom among newlyweds in our group, one either purchased or was given a gift of sterling silver flatware. In our case, we had difficulty settling on a pattern. Irv preferred an elaborate one and I chose a more modern, simple pattern. That being the case, we decided to postpone the purchase, bank the wedding gift fund, collect interest, until we would get together on a mutual choice of pattern. So we did. BUT- several years later the price of silver soared. All we could afford with the fund we had saved, were two lovely sets of stainless steel flatware, made in Italy, which we both liked. We never did purchase a set of sterling. The stainless steel served us well after all.

TRAVELING TOGETHER

Sometime after we were married, but before the children were born, we went on a cross country trip. We took the southern route going. We returned via the northern route through Canada. From today's perspective, the trip would be a challenge since we keep *kosher* (observing Jewish dietary laws). There was no saran wrap or aluminum foil yet. For the trip, our provisions from home included a roasted chicken, a salami and a dozen hard boiled eggs, a carton of wax paper, two thermos bottles and a container which had to be refilled with ice daily. The food lasted for a while. Thereafter, we stopped in A&P stores and asked the green market staff if we could wash the purchased vegetables in the back. We stopped milkmen at dawn, who were frequently driving horse and wagon. We asked them fill our two thermos bottles. They ladled the milk from large metal receptacles. The milk was usually foamy and cold. In towns we bought pints, yes pints, of ice cream and each of us consumed one. Books on tape were not available at the time. While Irv drove, I read aloud. We read about six books during our travels. When I wasn't reading, Irv serenaded me with a long repertoire of songs. He had an amazing memory for not only the lyrics, but the introductions as well. He kept me guessing the titles of the songs. Initially, when he sang the intros, I thought he was composing the lyrics! No car radios, he was better. There were no motels on the road. We stayed in rented cabins. They usually provided in addition to sleeping and bathroom accommodations, a two burner stove, a saucepan and a coffee pot. We would periodically hard boil a dozen eggs from local farms or the A&P. With canned tuna and salmon, eggs, cheese, bread and loads of fresh fruit and vegetables we sure "ate healthy".

Deborah and Irv on the road

We arrived at Yellowstone National Park the day it opened for the season. Snow covered the landscape. The roads were ploughed, but walls of snow, higher than the height of our car, were on either side. The hotel had not opened yet, so we rented one of the free standing cabins. It came with a pile of wood for the cabin's stove. We were advised to drain the water out of the auto's radiator to prevent freezing. After we were ready for bed, I had to go to the bathroom. You guessed it, there were no bathroom facilities in the cabin. They were in the shower house, not down the hall, but down a pathway some distance away. I put on several sweaters and a jacket and marched to the shower house. Halfway there, in front of me was a six foot or higher, black bear approaching me upright on two paws!!

I was petrified. So, s-l-o-w-l-y I turned and step by step, walked back to the cabin, with the bear following me. My heart was pounding. When I came into the cabin, Irv said, "Boy, that was quick. You sure went fast." I said that I didn't have to go anymore and told him about my unbearable venture. I haven't forgotten the experience more than sixty years later.

We left the amazing Yellowstone Park, having viewed its fantastic natural vistas, including the "timely" Old Faithful and the chocolate pudding - like, bubbling fountains. We next toured the Pinion Forest , where the pinion pines abound. We got out of our car at one point to see an enchanting landscape, bounded by a thicket of pinion pines. Instead of looking at the vista, I happened to glance down, at my feet. What did I see? A carpet of NUTS, mounds and mounds of small, beige nuts. At home we called them Indian nuts. The plethora of them was, as far as I was concerned, a real find. It could keep us busy cracking the shells, noshing all the way to the coast. What did I do? I returned to the car and retrieved two brown paper bags, (called "sacs" in some parts of the country) and diligently filled up both of them. I thought, "wow, this find would cost a fortune in our local appetizing store". So, off we drove. After a brief period, we decided to dig into our nutty larder. I took out one nut, and it was empty. Another, and wouldn't you know, it turned out to be empty too. Another and another and each one gave us the same empty result. We later found out that nuts that were on the ground had already been infiltrated and the kernels consumed by tiny worms! We had a supply of empty shells. In addition, we had a good laugh. Our nutty experience was a reminder of many happy moments and a pretext to retell and laugh.

When we returned from our cross country trip we were once again busy working, entertaining and involved in the community. From our early days together in Masada, Jewish affairs were important to us. We joined a local chapter of the American Jewish Congress. It was ideal: a dynamic multifaceted group of people with interest in the viability of Judaism, justice, civil rights, separation of church and state and support for the new state of Israel. Within a relatively short time, Irv assumed a leadership position. No matter which organization he joined, he usually ended up as president. The leadership was not sought by him, rather it was frequently thrust upon him. Irv was a very effective leader and public speaker. It was so in his practice as well. He served primarily as a litigator and was in court practically every day. He loved and thrived in his chosen profession. Irv did not seek fame or money. A substantial segment of his private practice was pro bono. He enjoyed helping and giving.

MY FATHER JACK

As I approach the retelling of the next stage, I find that I am reluctant to proceed. Is it that I have forgotten much, or rather that I am trying to repress the memories of painful experiences? I guess it's a bit of both. The process is impeding progress of the venture I've embarked upon: recording what I think I remember of my life and perhaps what I wish or should have forgotten.

As I mentioned before, my father was a gifted, creative artist. He taught me the love of being Jewish. The appreciation of creative items was passed on to me by him, whether on paper, sculpted in marble or crafted in metal, as well as the nuances of three dimensional works of art. He was a designer of jewelry, a metallurgist, manufacturer and very hard working individual. He named his firm "The Diamond Heart Company". He created a design for wedding bands which was patented. It was a series of hearts, one facing upward and the adjacent one downward, with a diamond in the center of each one. His firm was mentioned in the Readers Digest as one of the top three manufacturers of wedding rings in the 1930's. He adapted the lost wax method to casting gold and was a pioneer in casting platinum. His modus operandi: He designed a piece of jewelry, made the model, cast and finally finished the piece by hand. He experimented with fluxes, melting points, temperatures and timing in his kiln. It was hot, hard work and long hours.

My father Jack

During the war years soldiers bought gold wedding rings in the PX's and my father contributed to the supply. After he married Dora, he frequently did not go home, but slept in the office. He did not eat regularly. His food was ordered from a local kosher restaurant and Dora's brother picked it up. My father was a driven man, driven by Dora. She not only drove my father but my sister Evie as well. Evie was helping my father during some of her free time. She resented and hated being ordered around by Dora. Dora was a single-minded

93

taskmaster, bent on a successful business and earnings. No one would stand in her way. My father undoubtedly was aware of her behavior and acquiesced. He did not challenge or ever inject his views into the subtle and sometimes not so subtle, swirling family conflict.

Our lives were busy and fulfilling. Even though my father had a heart attack prior to his marriage to Dora, they led very active, busy lives. From my layman's perspective, he was working too many hours in the shop, on little sleep, following a poor diet, and very busy weekends with minimal rest.

One Sunday, as my Dad was driving in Westchester on one of their numerous, weekend, day trips, he had a second heart attack. He was taken to Mount Sinai hospital. After a few weeks, his recovery was presumably progressing satisfactorily. The morning of his pending discharge he had a massive heart attack. He died. We were told it was caused by a clot. I mention this because it was just a very short time before Coumadin came on the market. It was a painful time for all of us. He died just about ten years after our mother. My father was born on Feb. 29, 1896 and died on June 12, 1949; he was just 53 years old.

We now had a big job to do. His successful business had to be settled. My father left a will which stated that his assets to be equally divided among four heirs, my two sisters, Dora and myself. Dora went to court to contest the will, claiming that she was the wife of the deceased and was entitled to one third of the value of the estate. The law was on her side. It was not according to my father's intention or wishes. Since my father was in the high end jewelry business, most of his assets were located in the vault of his office. Dora was well acquainted with the office since she worked there before and after her marriage to my father. Before my father's funeral, unbeknownst to the three of us, Dora and her brother went to the vault in his office. They emptied his entire stock of diamonds, took gold and platinum jewelry including items designed by my father as gifts to my mother, which were to be given to the three of us. They did leave my mother's engagement ring and the personal jewelry which the three of us stored in the vault. It was a selective process.

Irving and I continued to live in the same house with Dora. Our relationship couldn't deteriorate much further, it had already reached bottom. Our only contacts involved the expenses regarding the house on East 5th street. Ronnie was living with Dora and it was increasingly uncomfortable for her, as my father was no longer there. So, shortly after he passed away, we moved her upstairs into our apartment, to our mutual delight and comfort. It was great having my baby sister living with us.

A few months after my father passed away, Dora married my father's good friend, a bachelor, Manny Friedlander.

BABY BOOMER BABIES

In the interim, Evie and David had accomplished a great deal. On Feb. 24, 1950 our baby niece, Freda Helen was born, starting a new generation. She monopolized the free time of the entire family. The apartment on Ocean Parkway became too small for the three of them. They purchased and moved to their newly built home in Green Acres in Valley Stream, Long Island. They were the pioneers in our family to move to the suburbs. We so enjoyed our baby niece; temptation was seeded.

Bubby and Poppa were also on an ongoing "nudging" campaign for a grandchild. Sometime in the beginning of 1951, Irv and I were about to plan a trip to Mexico and we also thought that maybe we should begin having a family. So we decided to flip a coin: heads would be "baby" and tails it would be a trip to Mexico. Heads came up. "Fertile myrtle", nine months later, gave birth to a baby boy. I had worked at JCCA up to the middle of the ninth month of my pregnancy.

On Sept. 12, 1951 I gave birth to Jack Avi Eiferman. He was named after my father, Jack. His middle name, Avi, in Hebrew means "my father". His Hebrew name was *Yaakov Avigdor*. Avigdor was his great-grandfather's name. So we all felt that in naming our first born, we satisfied the wishes of both sides of the family. What an adorable baby he was! He was the apple of his parents', grandparents' and family's eyes. He could easily have been spoiled, but he wasn't.

I was asked to stay on at JCCA, which was housed in a lovely brownstone on York Avenue on Manhattan's eastside. I was told that arrangements could be made for me to stay on working. Here was their plan: on pleasant days the baby could be left in the garden under supervision. Otherwise, one of the aides would watch him and call me, if needed. Since I was nursing him, I could express my milk and store it in the office refrigerator. Or, they would call me and I could nurse the baby. Taxi transportation could be arranged. It was amazing planning. However, I decided to stay home and enjoy our baby who was an utter delight.

Evie and David and Irv and I enjoyed our new status as parents. We had so much in common. By that time we had a car, a new, shiny, green Plymouth, which enabled us to get together most Sundays, frequently in Valley Stream.

Ronnie had graduated from Midwood High School and was away, enrolled at Syracuse University in upstate New York. She adored her baby nephew whenever she came home. We missed her when she was away at school. She was like our first grown up child as well as a beloved sibling. It was a good preparation for the future.

On May 6, 1952 another adorable niece was born, Norma Jean. All four of us "ooed" and "ahhed" over this lovable new baby Norma. We all relished the process and products of our growing families.

David, Norma, Evelyn, and Freda Wagner

I'm not sure exactly when, but in the 2nd half of her junior year or beginning of her senior year, Ronnie transferred to a college in New York City. I think it was Pratt Institute. In Syracuse she was popular and had many dates. One of the graduate students, Hillard Boss, was the lucky one chosen. A close relationship had developed and they were subsequently engaged to be married. Not only were they engaged, they wanted to get married very soon, as soon as Hilly was to leave for his first teaching position in Bainbridge, in upstate N.Y. The problem, as I saw it, was that Ronnie by then, had only one semester left to complete her degree. That didn't seem to matter to them. They wanted to get married NOW. Irv and I tried to convince them to take one of two options: 1) postpone getting married and Ronnie complete her senior semester in N.Y. After graduation they would marry and she would join Hilly in Bainbridge. Or 2) get married now and have a commuting marriage on weekends, while Ronnie completed her education on weekdays. They rejected both choices and opted to get married as soon as possible. Ronnie would quit college and they would take off to Bainbridge together. I was devastated, but there was little I could do. They were both adults and it was their life. For years and years thereafter, I kept trying to find programs and ways to convince Ronnie to complete her degree. To a certain extent, that would have also relieved me of the guilt of not fulfilling my mother's deathbed wish.

Ronya Berlinger and Hillard Boss, 1953

We all planned and arranged their lovely small wedding which was held at the Broadway Central on December 26, 1953. Irv and I and my fetus guided Ronnie down the aisle. Yep. I was in the fourth month of my pregnancy with our second child.

Our relationship with Ronnie, was in a way, in loco parentis. In her pre-marriage days Irv and I tended to insinuate our views and advice. So, before they were married Irv took Hilly aside for "fatherly advice". When they arrived at their honeymoon destination Hilly sent Irv a telegram: "ARRIVED SAFELY AWAITING FURTHER INSTRUCTIONS".

A few months later, on May 20, 1954, I gave birth to a blue-eyed adorable baby girl. We were thrilled. Irv had said: "She is my light." He thought he made up her name from the Hebrew word light, *(Ora)*. He would call her "Leora", to stand for "my light". "Oralee" just sounded too long and elaborate with Eiferman as a last name. So she was named Leora Freema Eiferman. Freema was after my mother's Hebrew name. Irv was sure he was the author of the name "Leora". We later discovered that Sinclair Lewis had used it as the name of a character in his novel "Arrowsmith"! It was also subsequently a very popular name for baby girls in Israel. So much for creative naming.

Raising a little girl, after a boy, was a new experience, but just as rewarding. Each time I gave birth, I was the only woman on the maternity floor in the hospital who was nursing her infant. I had little cooperation from anyone on the nursing staff. None of my friends nursed their babies. I was determined, with the encouragement of my obstetrician, to feed my baby the "old fashioned, tried and true" method. Initially, it was not easy. There was no "La Leche League" around at that time. The baby-nurse we hired to help me out wasn't on my side either. Apparently, one of the most satisfying activities for baby nurses is feeding the infant and I took that away from them. As an example: before I nursed Jackie the nurse took the baby from the crib, weighed him in his wet diaper and then gave him to me to nurse. Then she diapered him and weighed him again, scolding me that I didn't give him anything! She told me that I was starving my baby and he was not getting any sustenance from me! I was initially beside myself until I realized that I was being sabotaged. The baby-nurse did not last too long in our employ.

Jumping ahead in this litany, a few months ago, I was going through some of my records trying to "unclutter". I came across a few pages with a listing on each, with the following notations: e.g.

Sept. 26 - 6AM L R 20 min.

8AM R L 22 min.

9:45AM L R 18 min.

and the list went on and on for several pages. At first, I couldn't figure out what it was and why I had saved it. Since this paragraph follows the previous one, you can guess. It was a record of the times I nursed my infant son, which breast I started with and how long I nursed. I had developed my own method sans La Leche League. It was not an easy time. I recently shared the lists with the recipient and we had a good laugh. One of my idiosyncrasies is keeping records. It really is time for me to "unclutter". For the life of me I can't figure out why I ever saved them. However, they did serve as a reason to have a good laugh. Yes, I finally did throw them away along with a basketful of paper for recycling.

One of the treats Jackie enjoyed was pouring a little bit of ginger-ale into a glass of milk and watch it foam into a thick mixture. I remember once, when I was sitting in the "rocking nursing chair", nursing

Leelee, our nickname for Leora, three year old Jackie came by, shlepping behind him a liter bottle of ginger-ale along the floor, saying, "Give this to Leelee with your milk, it will taste better that way!"

Another time, when I was pregnant, Jackie wanted to know how and why babies were born. As part of my explanation, I told him "Daddy planted a seed" etc. He followed up with the question " Did Daddy use a hoe or a rake?"

I had made up my mind that, since our last name was so long, when we would have children, their first names would be short, never more than five letters. That decision was based on my childhood experience. My name, Deborah Berlinger, was sixteen letters long. As a child, in the early grades, I was still writing my name on the heading of the test paper, as the Friday morning weekly spelling words were already being dictated by the teacher. Since our eight letter last name couldn't be changed, we could keep the first name short. So we did.

On August 7, 1957 our youngest joy was born, finally after my third trip to the hospital. Each time I got there, my contractions ceased. After a while, I would be sent home. Every time I returned to the hospital I had to be prepped again and re-shaved! I was anxious to have my baby, but she was in no hurry. We were initially thinking of calling her "Sue", as her first name. Since her father was a lawyer, we later decided that "Sue Eiferman" wasn't such a funny or great idea. But we kept Sue as her middle name. Remembering the caveat, no more than five letters for a first name, we named our baby girl Loren Sue Eiferman.

Jack and Leora Have a New Baby Sister!

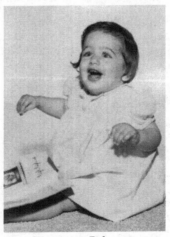

Loren as a Baby

The first night we brought her home, she slept

through the entire night. Irv and I were so apprehensive we periodically put a mirror in front of her tiny nose to be sure she was breathing. When she was born her long lashes reached the middle of her cheeks. Her fingernails were still attached to her tiny, thin long fingers. Perhaps she was waiting to finish her pre-natal development. She was a delight to raise.

One day when I took some garbage out to the pail in the alley at the side of the house, I found two sterling silver teapots and a sterling sugar bowl and cover in the pail! They were pieces from the eight or ten piece antique English, sterling silver tea set my father had given my mother as a gift! After my father passed away, I asked Dora about the tea set, which my father had said he wanted his daughters to have. She told me she didn't have it, wouldn't want it, and did not know where it was! Apparently, she preferred to dispose of it rather than letting us have it. Each of my sisters and I selected one piece from the "find". I still have the beautiful retrieved teapot.

Recalling the teapot incident brings another memory to mind. My father had an appreciation of the beauty that was artistically reflected in his exquisite jewelry designs and in a number of items he purchased at auctions. As a result, he had a few beautiful small sculptures on display in the reception room of his office. At home we also had some small sculptures with one large exception, Mary And Her Little Lamb.

It was a life size sculpture of a child, about four feet tall with a lamb at her side. She had a bonnet on. l loved the sculpture. It was carved in white Italian marble and placed on a marble pedestal. As a child, I always looked up at her. Years later, when I reached eye level, I appreciated the exquisite detail wrought by the sculptor. It was probably my favorite parents' possession. I grew up with Mary as a permanent fixture in our home. Mary remained in my father's apartment after he remarried. Dora compulsively directed Ronnie to clean every cranny and crevice of Mary monthly with Ivory Snow and a toothbrush. It drove Ronnie wild. After my father died, there was no way Dora would give or sell Mary to us. After Ronnie moved in with us we didn't know if the cleaning of Mary continued or what happened to Mary. I hope she ended up in a museum, where she really belonged.

A MEANINGFUL MOVE

Irving was committed to sending his children to public school. I, on the other hand, wanted them to have a Hebrew day school education. After much deliberation, Irv agreed to send our children to the Yeshivah of Flatbush.

Living in the same premises with Dora and her husband became increasingly upsetting. Irv and I decided to move. After much resistance, the house on East 5th street was sold. The proceeds were divided according to Dora's demands and legal right. She inherited one third and two thirds were divided among the three of us. Irv and I found a lovely one family home, on a dead end street just two blocks away from the Yeshivah of Flatbush, where Jackie was now enrolled. Some alterations were made on our new home. The bathroom was gutted and completely modernized and tiled, kitchen cabinet doors were refinished and windows were changed. I served as the contractor. We had minimal goof-ups and aggravation. The house had a slate roof, which I loved.

When our baby Loren was about one and a half years old, we moved from 777 East 5th street into our new home at 888 East 8th street. We were "coming up" in the world, not only numerically. I was delighted with the change.

888 East 8th Street Brooklyn

As soon as we moved, I took Loren to the top of the steps on the second floor, where our bedrooms were, and taught her to go down the steps backward on her belly. We repeated the process several times. She was an astute pupil and by the end of the second day she improved sliding down rapidly on her belly and pivoting with her hand and foot. As a result she would wait for us at the foot of the stairway as we descended in the traditional way!

In the interim, Ronnie and Hilly moved from Bainbridge to Poughkeepsie, N.Y. where Hilly had a new teaching position in the same town in which he grew up. Ronnie became the secretary in a department at Vassar College. I seem to remember that it was in the English Department. That was followed by a social studies position for Hilly on Long Island. At their request, before they moved, Evie and I scouted out a home for them. We found a house we all fell in love with in Rockville Center, Long Island. It was a magical house designed by or built for an actor. The bedrooms were off a balcony on the second floor, reminiscent of the Shakespearian period. The house had many hidden nooks and crannies. The architecture and design of the exterior of the house was in the Tudor style.

On December 30, 1957 Ronnie gave birth to Michael Daven Boss, just four months after Lori was born. Three years later, on Nov. 16, 1960, Julie Ann Boss, Michael's baby sister, was born. They were lovable. It was a feeling of joy that my baby sister had become this wonderful loving wife and mother. The three sisters shared much, from child raising advice a la Dr. Spock, to the constant interchange of cartons of children's clothing. It was wonderful having our expanding families, with the ages of the children close enough so that, to this day, the cousins have remained close. As young adults they contact each other on an ongoing basis.

The Boss Family
Julie, Hill, Robyn Talman, Mike, and Ronnie Boss

I embarked upon this opus for my children, grandchildren and family members, so that they will know something about our family's history. I wrote about some events they may recall, to highlight them from my perspective, or to serve as a reminder.

Each of our children attended the Yeshivah of Flatbush. Snippets of some things I recall: When Jackie was in first grade, his teacher told me he was staring out the window and obviously was not paying attention. She called on him. He told her that he was flying in outer space and she would just have to wait until he got back! Another time, when he was in second or third grade, a mother of one of the students in his class, met me as I was shopping on Avenue J. She asked me why I had not been in school that morning to see the class play. It was adorable and Jackie was great. He had the main role! Jackie never gave me the invitation. When I later asked him about it, he said he had a good time. After a serious discussion, it was agreed that I would be given any and every communication the school sent home.

When Leora was in third grade she dreamed in Hebrew. On a number of occasions I would hear her speak Hebrew in her sleep. She was so steeped in the language that she thought in Hebrew at times. In eighth grade she was sent home from school by the English Department principal, Mr. Weiss, because her skirt was too short. We lived only two blocks away from the school. She was told to go home, change and report back to him. Leora came home borrowed one of my skirts which reached her ankles. She held it up at her waist with a large diaper pin. She then walked back to his office and said: "Is this long enough?" The principal burst out laughing and said: "O.K., O.K., you made your point". She said she laughed along with him.

Loren, unlike her siblings, from her toddler days on, was always able to keep herself busy with a multifaceted array of play and art activities. She was a busy, active loner.

While Jack and Leora were attending elementary school, I was very involved and active in the Ladies Auxiliary, which in the Yeshivah, was equivalent to a parent teachers association (PTA). Not having a babysitter, Lori came with me. The Hebrew principal, Mar Braverman, knew me as a child. He would frequently pick Loren up and say she was as special to him as if she was his own grandchild. He was the founder of the school, and had no children of his own, and in some respects, he considered the students his children. Since my parents were no longer alive, Lori believed, at one point, that he was indeed her grandfather!

Many, if not most, of my peers had a mink coat. One day, I casually mentioned to Irv that "I would like to have a fur coat one of these days". Irv responded with a big smile, "You already have one; it walks to the Yeshivah every day!" Although the tuition was no longer $30 a month, as it was when I attended, with three children getting a Yeshivah education, the tuition bills did impact our family budget.

Periodically Irv and I took off weekends and went away. The children were dropped off at Evie and David's home. At other times Freda and Norma were our guests and Evie and David took off. It worked out beautifully. The cousins enjoyed each other's company and the vacationing parents had a two day treat.

One memorable vacation we took was a week-long cruise on the Queen Elizabeth or the Queen Mary, I can't remember which, on its maiden voyage to Aruba. Bubby and Poppa stayed with the children. I prepared fifteen lunches. The brown paper bags were each filled with an apple, a cookie and a napkin. All fifteen bags were lined up along the kitchen counter. The sandwiches were refrigerated. Dinners were refrigerated and/or frozen. Jackie prepared breakfast for the family and for his grandparents as well. Leora and Loren had clearing and cleaning responsibilities. The children had been trained and rehearsed. Jackie organized the chore charts and supervised. Irv's parents complained that there was little for them to do! When we returned, the report was that the children were wonderful. We had a ball. Since Aruba was a free port we purchased our Spode dinnerware there. We selected the fleur de leis pattern and bought service for twelve so that each of the children could, in time, inherit service for four. It seemed like an illogical decision about a distant future. At this stage, I'm beginning to think it was a good idea after all.

After graduation from elementary school, Jackie went on to a public high school, Midwood, where he gained a positive sense of his academic abilities. He had a new circle of great friends. Although the Yeshivah administration tried to encourage Leora to attend Hebrew high school, she chose to follow her brother to Midwood. Some years later Loren followed suite. Irv became involved in Midwood High School's PTA. He was president of the PTA for a number of years. It was during the time when parents were enfranchised and had a significant role

113

in hiring the administrators of the school. Irv appeared frequently at the NYC Board of Education hearings. He was involved in the choice, and eventual hiring, of the principal of Midwood High School. In June of 1975, when Lori was still a student there, Irv was awarded an honorary diploma from Midwood High School at the graduation ceremony. He was told that he was the oldest individual who ever received a diploma from Midwood!

We had a delightful custom on our block on East 8th street, in Brooklyn. If the weather was nice, from warm Spring days through early Fall, we would sit outdoors in front of our homes, along with our neighbors and have a post dinner social gab fest. After the dishes were done, Irv and I would spend evenings outdoors with our next door neighbor, Mr. Sternberg. Current events, theatre, and politics were all on the agenda. Mr. Sternberg was a bright chemical engineer with an exhaustive fund of knowledge. He sometimes entertained us with his musical renditions on the mandolin. Once in a while, Mrs. Sternberg joined in our get-togethers. Mr. S. had a portable radio. On April 17, 1961 we were all glued to his radio, listening to President Kennedy speaking to the nation about the Bay of Pigs disaster. We were experiencing fear and apprehension. It was vibrantly visible at our doorstep, listening and experiencing history.

Another time history was etched on my memory.

It was July 20, 1969. I was standing in our library with Bubby watching TV as Neil Armstrong landed and walked on the moon. When I explained to Bubby what was happening, she just waved her hand in her characteristic dismissive gesture and said it was just a make believe movie. To the day she passed away, I don't think she believed we had landed a human on the moon.

JACK'S BAR MITZVAH

When it came time to plan Jack's Bar Mitzvah we decided that we wanted to focus on a meaningful, religious and spiritual experience. We therefore decided not to have an elaborate "catered affair" in celebration of his Bar Mitzvah *aliya* (call up to the Torah) and instead take the family to Israel. When we returned from the trip he would have a 13th birthday party for all his classmates in our finished basement. We would follow that with a series of dinner parties at home for friends and family. Jack's Hebrew birthday that year was in late August. We planned a month's trip to Israel. The children did not miss any school time. Irv arranged a month away from his practice. We had hoped that Evie and Ronnie and their families would join us. However none of them could manage to get away. The five of us and Poppa and Bubby made the trip. In addition, a number of our friends and their families were planning to go to Israel that summer. They joined us for the Bar Mitzvah and a luncheon following services. We coordinated our travel plans and stayed at the same hotels. The children even had their friends with them for part of the time.

Rav Shach, Jack's teacher in the Yeshivah, came from Israel and was with us during our stay. He was very helpful in planning our itinerary and making arrangements. Jack had to be tested before the main synagogue, Heychal Shlomo, would permit him to be called to the Torah for his *aliyah*. He passed with flying colors. Jack was the first American who had a Bar Mitzvah in Israel after the State was declared. We still did not have access to the Western Wall. Jerusalem was a divided city. They were so impressed with Jack's preparation and performance, they said from now on, any Yeshivah of Flatbush student could have a Bar Mitzvah there without being tested.

Poppa's nephew, Max Halpern, lived in Kibbutz Kfar Masaryk with Rivkah and his family. We spent some time with them in the Kibbutz and invited them to the Bar Mitzvah in Jerusalem as our guests. We also had a number of friends who had made *aliyah* over the years. They were invited as well. Rav Shach and his mother-in-law were helpful in arranging for the luncheon we hosted in the President Hotel, where we were staying. We chose that hotel because, at the time, it was one of the only ones that had a swimming pool with mixed gender swimming! After a hot time touring, it was great to dunk.

At the services in the synagogue, Jack sat between the Minister of Religion and some other government official. The women sat overlooking the proceedings in the balcony, several stories above. When Jack looked up at his sisters and me there was an audible "ayyyys" from the female congregation. He chanted his portion skillfully and confidently. We were so proud of him. Truthfully, I could barely see him through my tear filled eyes. But, I did hear him loud and clear! When I read and heard the words in the *sidur* (prayer book") : " *Kee meetzione taytzay Torah...*" (From Zion the Torah.....) I had goose pimples, I could not believe it. Here I was in Jerusalem, for the first time in my life, on a *Shabbat* (Sabbath), hearing the Torah read! It was an emotional and spiritual moment I clearly remember more than fifty years later.

Jack's *Bar Mitzvah*
Heychal Shlomo, Jerusalem
From left: Irving, Loren, Jack, Leora, Deborah

At the same time, unbeknownst to us, twenty French orphans from Paris were invited by the government to have a mass Bar Mitzvah at Haychal Shlomo the same day. One boy read the *barachah* (prayer) on behalf of all of them. We invited all the boys to join us for the luncheon at the hotel after services. The hotel staff was great in making the last minute arrangements successfully. The French boys didn't know English and understood little Hebrew and Jack did not speak French. Yet they did seem to have a good time together dancing the Horah. Our children and most of the guests also joined in the dancing. That was followed by a delicious meal, singing and a lot of humming. The function was held in a lovely spot overlooking the pool.

We did a great deal of touring the parts of Israel that were accessible. Jerusalem was, as I mentioned, a divided city. There were times when our tour ended, when we were faced with, and blocked by, a bullet pocked wall. Our guide was Rav Shach's brother-in-law, whom I recall, was a botany professor at Hebrew University. The touring was phenomenal. He had the children act out parts of the Bible on site: e.g. as we came to the valley of Elah (*Nahal ha'Elah*) one of the children was asked to portray Goliath, the other acted as David. Another time, at Eyn Gedi, the children climbed into a cave; one of them assumed the role of Saul, the other David. Other times he would pick up a leaf or weed, have us taste or smell it, one was spicy, another salty. He then quoted or told us where in the Bible the name of the plant was mentioned. Our family sat, depending on our perspective or position, in or on the Dead Sea. Irv read the newspaper sitting, not walking, on water. We took a trip to the Negev and some of us snorkeled in Eilat. We visited Ophera, which at that time was just being settled. There was only a gas station, a one room bank and a small shop which sold drinks and some fruit. We filled the gas tank and bought a watermelon. During the intervening years, the "Ophera stop" sure has grown and changed into a city. On our trip back to Jerusalem, the van's stick- shift got stuck in second gear. We were very lucky to have the *"mellohn"* (melon) from Ophera. Not having any water left, it lubricated our parched throats. There was no air-conditioning. We finally, very s-l-o-w-l-y arrived back in Jerusalem late that night!

WONDERFUL WAUBEEKA

Some thirty-five or forty years ago we found the "country home" we had been seeking for some time. For years I had stored away dishes and other items which would be perfect for our future vacation home. We looked at the Shinnecock Hills section in the Hamptons and rejected it because the trip, on a weekend on the Long Island Expressway, was too heavily trafficked and long. Next, was an offer from Irv's friend, Al Raditch, of some land not far from Tanglewood, if we found eight other couples who would be interested in joining and build homes there. We found some interested friends, but before we made a commitment to join, we made the trip to the desirable area. Apparently many other couples found the area desirable too. The weekend traffic on Route 7 was stop-and-go, so this venture turned out to be a no-no too. So much for the Tanglewood area.

We almost gave up the idea of finding a vacation home when a neighbor in Brooklyn, Mike Banks, told us he knew of a place not too distant, which he thought might be of interest. It was located less than two hours away, at the foothills of the Berkshires. The community was founded by the *Ner Tormid* (eternal light) Society, a group of Jewish New York City firemen. There were about 180 homes surrounding a 52 acre natural lake with coves and a peninsula, in a private, gated, 606 acre community. Some homes dotted the tree lined lake, and there were "forever wild" areas surrounding the Lake Waubeeka community. Each person we visited, including Mike's cousin, Henry Nussbaum, claimed they had the best spot on the mountain. Everyone loved the community. There was also a small synagogue on the premises built by hand by a group of the founders. Waubeeka sparked our interest, if we could find a house for sale bordering the lake. As we were leaving we saw a "for sale by owner" sign on a property on the lake! A man was standing in front. The house was small, white and asbestos shingled. The area had lovely rock outcroppings and trees surrounded by flowers between the adjacent houses. I said to the man, " If those rock and flower outcroppings belonged to the house for sale, we would be interested". He replied, "Well, it doesn't belong to me." That did it! I told Irv that even if the house was terrible, (it turned out to be), time, creative ideas, money and patience could make the house lovely. But nothing could change the property or the location and that was what attracted us. Irv copied the contact information down and so our happy vacation home venture began.

Irv contacted the owner and after deliberations a contract was signed. We would rent the house at an agreed fee for six months, from September to

February, with the option to buy. A price was agreed upon. If we purchased the house, the rental payments would go toward the payment of the house. I was so pleased with the agreement my beloved lawyer negotiated. Renting and living in the house part time for six months gave us a realistic idea of what had to be done and also acquainted us with the Danbury area. It was just before the real estate bubble and coincided with the week we paid off the mortgage of our home in Brooklyn. I worked Thursday nights instead of Fridays. Our routine was to leave Brooklyn late Thursday night, after I finished work at Brooklyn College and spend the weekend in Waubeeka. Irv arranged to take Fridays off. We returned to Brooklyn Sunday, late afternoon, all through the Fall and Winter. The first summer we lived in Waubeeka we were offered, unsolicited, double the purchase price. Over the years, we have since invested in three major alterations, way over double the price we had paid. We continue to enjoy Lake Waubeeka. The approach to the community, as one turns off Route 7 on to Starrs Plain road, used to be a steep dip in the road. As we descended into the depression, each time, I felt almost every muscle in my body relax. It was an automatic response. Waubeeka has been a place where our family and friends congregate, where we relax, entertain and, above all, have established and maintained friendships. We attend all Jewish holidays at Lake

Waubeeka, in our small Congregation Mount Moses. By the way, on the official U.S. geodetic map, the name of the mountain on which Waubeeka is located is "Mount Moses". How appropriate.

POPPA AND BUBBY

We visited Irv's parents frequently, and they often came over to our home. Irv's father, Joseph, was called "Poppa" by the children. He was outgoing and affectionate. He was the owner and supervisor of a police uniform manufacturing company prior to his retirement. He was also the president of a *landsmanschaft* organization, the "Nadworna Young Men's Benefit Association", for many years until its dissolution. It was an organization founded by and for immigrants from the same European town, *Nadworna*. They provided support, financial, social and burial plots for their members.

"Bubby", Sarah, Irv's mother, on the other hand was a quiet individual, reserved and shy. Poppa died February 14, 1969. We missed him very much. We felt that Bubby needed help and we were not comfortable having her live alone. We arranged for help in her home several times with different individuals. She was not pleased with having anyone and kept dismissing each of them. After a while, we decided to have her live with us, since hired assistance was not working out.

When we moved into our four bedroom home on East 8th street, I knew that someday one of Irv's parents would come to live with us. Therefore we initially divided the rooms accordingly: Irv and I had the master bedroom, Jackie had the small bedroom, the large bedroom was shared by both girls, and the fourth bedroom became the TV and den, awaiting the time when a grandparent would join us. I did not want any of the children to feel, in the future, that they were losing their space and room when one of Irv's parents moved into our home.

The girls, Leora and Loren, shared a bedroom, sometimes cooperatively and other times not. At one point they hung a large piece of fabric, I think it was a bedspread, across the room. They computed the dividing line, inch by inch.

One time, when I came into their room, the mess and clutter on Leora's side needed attention. I read the riot act to her, and told her she had to clear her room pronto. About twenty minutes later Leora came downstairs to the kitchen, smiling. "All done", she declared. I went upstairs and indeed, surfaces were cleared and not a smidgen of clutter visible! Later, that evening I went to put the garbage out at the side of the house, and lo and behold, the contents of drawers, including her Bat Mitzvah jewelry box and its contents, rolls of stamps, socks, etc. were dumped into the pail! My daughter had emptied some of her drawers and many of her possessions to "clear the way". To this day, Leora does get attached to people, but not to "things". She is not nostalgic. I think, perhaps, its her reaction to my not throwing things away.

Since I was born during Depression years, I keep or store away many items, finding or hoping to find a future use for them. I still tend to save glass jars, rubber bands, string, wrapping paper, gift boxes and more. I'm the original recycler. I have no difficulty "giving away", but "throwing out" is not easy.

Much to Bubby's disappointment, she moved in with us and the TV den was transformed into her bedroom. The one disadvantage was that there was a full flight of steps to negotiate every day. She managed like a trouper. In retrospect, I do not feel that she was ever happy with the move, even though she had led a very isolated, lonely life before. She had not cultivated any friends long before Poppa's death. She never went out alone or shopped on her own. Her social life was conducted by, and revolved around, Poppa. As I had indicated, she was a very private and shy individual. I was told that as a young girl she came to the United States alone and on her own. That must have taken guts! She did not like living here and went back to Europe! That took even a greater degree of guts. She met Poppa in Europe and they married. When Irv was two months old Bubby sailed back to the United States with Poppa and their baby. I can barely conceive of how difficult it must have been sailing in steerage

127

with an infant. That took guts again!

Poppa and Bubby in Europe
Sarah Sobel and Joseph Eiferman

Poppa and Bubby in our home in Brooklyn

It's odd how memories of years seem to slide by and are perhaps consigned to oblivion. Yet some moments of the past surface randomly in photographic clarity. One such photo shot is on a Spring day. I returned from class and found Bubby

128

sitting adjacent to the lawn in front of our home, animatedly engaged in conversation with our Italian gardener. She was complaining to him that her husband had deserted her. She was speaking in Yiddish and the gardener was talking in Italian! Although neither one understood the other, perhaps each one was getting something off their chest. By the way, my father-in-law did not desert her, he died. I guess, to her it was equivalent to desertion.

Bubby was distracted by and involved with our children. She exerted and displayed some control over the most vulnerable, Loren, the youngest. Unbeknownst to me, when no one else was around, she periodically ordered Loren around. Although Loren was unhappy about it. She never complained or mentioned it to us. She just tolerated the situation graciously. It was years later, after Bubby passed away, that I found out.

BACK TO WORK

Loren was not the only one who reacted to Bubby living with us. I attribute some of my motivation to working and going back to school, was to getting away from home. After volunteering forty some odd hours a week in the Yeshivah, I realized that I had time to resume my career, after all. I went back to school during several summers in order to get away as well as to renew and upgrade my professional skills. When I left volunteering and went to work, my peers accused me of being a "deserter". Most of the women in our circle were "stay-at-home" mothers. I was a certified guidance counselor, having passed the city Board of Education and the New York State exams in 1969.

I began working as a guidance counselor in a public school on a part time basis. Guidance counseling was a relatively new area. The school I was assigned to never had a guidance program before. That presented a happy challenge. I arrived at the school, P.S. 208, to meet with the principal, Dr. Ordan, and to be interviewed by him. A well groomed man, in suit and tie, greeted me in his first floor tiny office. I assumed he was the principal. He graciously asked me to wait. Puzzled, I waited. He then escorted me up to the second floor to meet Dr.

Ordan. My escort was the superintendent of the building!

Working with Dr. Ordan was both professionally and personally enhancing. He was bright, cooperative, perceptive and had a "hands on" modus operandi with his staff and students. He was delighted to have a guidance program established in the school. I also set up a circulating library of guidance books and materials for pupils, staff and parents. In addition to the pupils, in grades 1 to 8, I had numerous and ongoing contacts with teachers as well as parents.

One incident I recall always brings a smile. Dr. Ordan, the principal, was away for the day. The assistant principal, Stanley Friedman, was in charge. Mid-morning I was summoned to the principal's office and told it was an emergency. A parent, a City Councilman, whom I had previously met, had been called in because his son was having discipline difficulties. Both the father and son were in the office. The assistant principal greeted me outside the office door, obviously stressed and steered me in. I went in and he closed the door behind me, remaining outside! I walked in and there was a short, stocky man in his thirties, waving his pants belt over his head in circles, cursing his little third grade son, who, petrified, was cowering before him. The whizz of the revolving belt was audible, as were his colorful, vivid curses." I'm gonna knock the daylights outa you, you little xxxx". He was a wild, infuriated man. I walked in on this scene. What to do? No guidance course prepared me for this. "Deborah", I said to me, "diffuse, distract this". So, with all the gumption I could muster, I began to laugh, and called out, "Mr. X ", I called him by name, "your pants are falling down!!" (They weren't.) He stopped swinging his pants belt in mid air, looked down, then at me – and began to laugh! He threaded his belt, buckled it, and subsequently we had a "guidance conference".

COLLEGE CAREER

I loved working at P.S. 208. But, once again, I realized that I preferred to deal with older students and adults. So, I began to apply to Brooklyn College for a position. I had sent in my resume to Brooklyn College, applying for a counseling position, probably three or four times. It's been said that timing is everything. Lo and behold my last resume arrived at the very same time that one of the counselors was handing in her resignation! It also was helpful that a staff member who knew of me, Estelle Ritchin, was present. From then on I was a "shoe in". I met the qualifications. I regretfully left my co-workers at the elementary school and happily embarked on my college career. I initially worked part time, four nights a week, from 6 to 10 P.M. We worked out the family's schedule. I served an early dinner. Each of the children had revolving responsibilities clearing and cleaning up. Irv arranged to be home in the evenings. By the following semester I had a full time faculty position, working four days a week with only one night assignment. Eventually I had a line appointment and achieved tenure.

DOCTORAL DEGREE

Having a faculty position at the college, I realized that I had a professional obligation to continue my own education and so I embarked on finding and then qualifying for a doctoral degree. In my search, I would take a course in the university I was considering. My first inclination was to enroll in Yeshivah University and so I did. However, I didn't care for their program and their administrative and departmental practices. I tried courses in a number of other universities that offered doctoral programs in counseling. I ended up at Fordham University. I was, I think, the oldest or near oldest student in the program. Working full time at Brooklyn College and attending Fordham after work, three nights a week, eliminated a good chunk of my free time. The family was very cooperative and encouraging. I will admit that Bubby and the subsequent desire to get away were also motivating factors. In order to accommodate my work and family responsibilities, I never enrolled in full-time programs. I usually only took one or two courses at a time. I recall how getting research papers done was difficult to fit into my schedule.

One of the requirements for the doctoral program was to take a foreign language or a statistics course. I opted for the foreign language. Throughout my academic career I have avoided math and music whenever possible. Perhaps if I ever applied myself to these areas I would not be intimidated by them. It's sort of late at this stage to start. Initially I thought my thesis would involve *mussar* (ethics) and moral development with Hebrew Day School students as the subjects. Therefore, Hebrew was the logical foreign language. The big plus was that I knew and had taught the language. A Fordham professor had to test my proficiency in Hebrew. The test was to be administered at Rose Hill, the Bronx campus. The priest who tested me seemed to be nervous. I felt confident of my ability in Hebrew. He handed me an old flaking text, the edge of the pages were brittle and yellowed. The text was from an obscure commentary on the geography of the land and rivers of ancient Persia. I had no difficulty translating. I realized that he did not know modern Hebrew. He had not responded to anything I had said to him in Hebrew before he tested me. I sympathized with him. He was assigned this task and I guess he was only acquainted with Hebrew by researching ancient texts. In any event he seemed uncomfortable throughout the procedure. I found it a breeze.

For my dissertation I researched the potential effect of education on the moral development and dogmatism of adult college students. Many individuals helped, supported and encouraged me along the multi year project. My cousin, Dr. Ruth Myer, a psychologist, who was working in Washington at the time, helped me design the tests I administered. Dr. Ira Perell assisted with the statistical aspect. Dr. Louis Nulman's nascent recommendations influenced the design of the research proposal. The subjects were a group of adult college students and staff personnel served as the control group. They were great. My three children were amazingly cooperative, interested and helpful. I also approached them as sounding boards and to score some of the tests that were administered. Above all, Irv was there "all the way", as a partner and a reliable source of encouragement.

Fordham Graduation, 1979 PhD

Since I was working full time and concurrently working on my doctorate, when it came to the

Passover holiday we opted to observe and celebrate the holiday away at a hotel. And indeed, away we went. In addition to our clothing, I packed cartons of books and papers. While the rest of the family went swimming, playing and taking advantage of the hotel facilities, I was in our room without having to deal with work or household and holiday responsibilities. Rather, I was reading, writing and studying full time. It was a productive period.

Working on my thesis was, at times, an all consuming process. Creative periods were intermittent. Sometimes they came about at two or three o'clock in the morning or while I was jogging either on Ocean Parkway in Brooklyn, or by Lake Waubeeka in Connecticut. I dutifully recorded the ideas as I cooled down from my jog. When a great idea came to me at the lake, I would mentally refer to it as my "Lake of Diamonds". For indeed as the sun shone on the lake's surface it sparkled like a sheet of gems. To this day, over 35 years later, I think of the lake as my "Lake of Diamonds".

As I said before, creative spurts came in my sleep. After reworking my thoughts I would be so pleased with the fabric of my woven words. On awakening by the morning light, the creative ideas that came to me in the middle of the night, were merely evanescent wisps of dreamed "gems". Efforts to retrieve them inclined to be exercises in futility. I was so frustrated. I felt as if my forgotten thoughts were lost treasures. So, one night I decided to experiment. I placed a pen and pad on the night table adjacent to my side of the bed. As soon as I was semi aware in my sleep that I was in "creative mode", I immediately jotted the thoughts down. Great idea! Next morning, as soon as I opened my eyes, I went to my notepad. Pages and pages were filled from top to bottom with wiggly lines resembling a cardiogram! Alas, the conceived thoughts, ideas and commentaries were lost, never to be duplicated in script or print. So much for my experimenting.

My advisors at the university were many. My first one passed away and my second one was hospitalized. I decided that I would try to select as my next advisor, a younger individual who would be too old to go on maternity leave. I selected a female advisor who subsequently left the university to go away, I think, with her newly married spouse. I was told that she left without even collecting her final paycheck. She also left with my dissertation, awaiting her final signature of approval! I had to hire a detective agency to find her. We finally were able to retrieve my signed dissertation. My last advisor, Dr. Herman Slotkin, was an unremitting mentor as I achieved my goal. When it finally came down to taking my orals, a member of my committee suggested that I should do some additional research on one aspect. I told him I thought it was a great idea and invited him to do it with me after I graduate. I did graduate after nine long years. Yep, it took nine years to achieve my doctorate and only nine months to have each of my wonderful children.

VARIOUS VENTURES

Professionally, in addition to my full time position, I was busy delivering papers in different parts of the country, attending and chairing some conferences, as well as writing proposals for guidance programs. I was also a recipient of a number of awards relating to both my academic and community activities. Most conferences involved travel. Irv always accompanied me on these ventures. I vividly remember a conference held in Potsdam, N.Y., not the one with the Big Three (Truman, Churchill and Stalin in 1945) but in the same location. We arrived at the hotel by car, late in the afternoon, when I suddenly realized that I had left the bag with my shoes at home. I was scheduled to deliver a paper the next day. I had a lovely new business suit to wear and only the pair of formerly white old sneakers that I had on! What to do? We quickly rushed into the small downtown area and caught the owner of the only shoe store in town as he was closing his door for the evening. We implored him to reopen and shod me with a new pair of shoes. He complied. Thereafter, I enjoyed wearing the shoes, especially when I recalled the circumstance of the purchase. The delivery of the paper was also a success.

At Brooklyn College I served on a number of committees and was the faculty advisor to Encore, a club composed of adult students who had resumed their education. They were a fascinating, interesting group, who as individuals, continued to enhance my time as their advisor.

In addition to matters relating to my college work, Irv and I were both active in the community. Irv had positions of leadership in a number of organizations. For example, in addition to the PTA of Midwood High School, he was the Brooklyn borough president of the American Jewish Congress as well as a member of its national Governing Council.

Irv and I, along with Rabbi Jerry and Lila Karlin, and Gloria and Jerry Greenman, were involved in founding the GET organization. GET stood for "Getting Equitable Treatment". We worked to help women, on an individual basis, secure a Jewish divorce (*Get*) from recalcitrant spouses. Using social work guidelines, I set up and trained our corps of volunteer social workers to help the *agunot*, the women who were (chained) in their unhappy marriages. We meticulously observed the confidentiality of those who turned to us for help. We met once a week and worked concurrently with our "clients", individual rabbis, as well as rabbinical organizations. Primarily women turned to us, and occasionally a man. Most of our clients lived in the

NYC area. A handful came from all parts of the country, Israel, Canada and Britain. We produced and distributed throughout the country a brochure describing the steps to form similar groups. The GET organization was probably one of the first modern such groups to address the problem of *agunot*. Today, there are myriad groups and individuals working with the victims in an effort to solve this pervasive, religious problem. After many years, despite helping a significant number of *agunot* receive their *gittin* (Jewish divorces), I was burned out and left the GET organization. My friendship with Gloria Greenman continues.

When Irv passed the Bar he initially worked for Schenley's. That was followed by a stint with Mr. Kramer, a Brooklyn lawyer in private practice. Thereafter, he was on his own. He had a general practice and served as a litigation attorney in court practically every day. He loved it. The variety, from criminal, including murder, to landlord tenant, to civil and matrimonial cases all enhanced his enjoyment and devotion to his profession. Frequently he worked on a pro bono basis. I recall him saying at times that one of his clients was having a tough time and it just made sense to forget about the fee. He never, in all the years he was in practice, mentioned a client by name or identified them to me. As an example: I once got a call from my sister Evie, informing me that the four of us were going out for dinner the next day, to celebrate. When I asked her what we were celebrating, she told me Irv won the case he had been handling for her the past four months. He had never mentioned it to me. He meticulously observed the confidentiality of his clients, including my sister.

Although David and Irving were only brothers-in-law, not brothers, their relationship was not only congenial but loving as well. Sometime in the 60's or 70's David developed acromegaly. His facial features gradually changed and enlarged. He remained the same outgoing, articulate person with a wonderful sense of humor. Some years later he was stricken with kidney cancer. Toward the end of his devastating illness he said that he wanted to be at home, not in the hospital. Indeed, he died at home with his wife and daughters at his bedside on January 20, 1979, at the age of fifty six. Oh, we missed him so much.

As I indicated, I'm not going to be either chronological or detailed about events that "the children" remember. Our perspectives vary. I will just give my recollections regarding a number of incidents or events that may amplify, be forgotten or be of interest. Then again, they may not be, but so it goes.

SISTERS WEEK

Ronnie, Debbie, and Evie, 1980

My sisters Evelyn, Ronya and I had been close during all of our adult years. Sometime during a summer in the late 70's or early 80's, Ronya had surgery. It was decided that it would be best if she spent her recovery with me in Lake Waubeeka since there were only a few steps in our house. The additional incentive was that we could have the unique opportunity to spend quality time together. It not only turned out to be a successful recovery, it was the beginning of a family tradition. Evelyn joined Ronya and me. We decided to spend a week together each summer at Lake Waubeeka, without our husbands. We called it "Sisters Week". It was a wonderful, fantastic and enjoyable week for the three of us. We visited area attractions, museums, parks, saw plays, etc. We reminisced, giggled and had a ball. Some nights we would be up to all hours. It was like being teen agers all over again. It was a remarkable opportunity to be together, without having family and household responsibilities, appreciating and loving each other for one precious week a year. Our husbands were not happy about our annual sororal venture. Over the years we had many delightful, unforgettable experiences.

The Sisters at Loren and Joe's House, 1994

For example, one rainy morning during Sisters Week, we decided to take our daily walk in the nearby Danbury Mall. Another unanimous decision was that we would walk together and we would **not** shop. To guarantee this, we left our purses in the locked car. We walked round and round and on one of the rotations we glanced in the window of one of the clothing shops at an attractive display of T-shirts. You guessed it, we went in. We each chose a T-shirt we liked and tried it on in the individual private fitting rooms. When it came to processing the purchases we realized we had no money! We left the packaged shirts at the desk, went back to the parking lot, retrieved our wallets and returned to conclude the purchase. When we got back to Lake Waubeeka we showed our purchases to each other. From the myriad of colors and styles each of the Berlinger "girls" chose three duplicate shirts! We are sisters in many ways. Those memorable and significant Sisters Weeks continued for 15 more years.

Lake Waubeeka, July 1995

For a long time, I periodically became compulsive in trying to find ways my sister Ronnie could complete her baccalaureate. I investigated, computed, and cajoled; I checked into her taking courses in non traditional venues, or completing her senior year in absentia. I computed and maximized her transfer credits in a number of institutions, to no avail. I had failed in fulfilling my mother's dying request. The unfulfilled promise to my mother kept niggling me, not Ronnie.

When Ronnie was approaching her late sixties, she was living in Amherst, in an academic milieu. She finally applied to U. Mass. at Amherst, completed her course work, and did graduate, summa cum laude! When she invited us to her graduation ceremony she said that she wanted to share the diploma with me. My silent, thankful prayer that night was, "Mom, Ronnie graduated and she fulfilled your dying wish."

As I am hunt- and- pecking away, I realize that chronology and memories are fusing. Once again, am I writing a memoir or an autobiography? Perhaps I should refer to it as a "memoirography". According to the New Oxford American Dictionary "Autobiography" is defined as "an account of a person's life written by that person". "Memoir" is defined as "a historical account or biography written from personal knowledge", or "an autobiography or written account of one's memory of certain events or people". I don't see the difference. I'm writing either one or both. Have your choice.

MARRIAGES AND CONSEQUENCES

When Jack was a high school senior I would frequently come home and find Fern Alexander on our front steps, waiting for Jack to come home. It was a portend of a future relationship.

They were married in their early twenties. An elaborate wedding, on December 30, 1972, was hosted by the Alexanders and us. It was a color coordinated ceremony. Loren and Leora were among the bridesmaids as well as Cinda, Fern's sister. Her sister Stacey was maid of honor. My gown was custom made by a gifted Broadway costume designer. It was brown velvet. The V-neck was trimmed in white ermine as were the cuffs. It was a copy of a gown worn by an English Queen several centuries ago. The gown was beautiful and worn once! I'm not quite sure how we were inveigled to have such an elaborate affair. I guess since it was the first of the Alexander's three daughters to be married, they wanted to have an "extravaganza". It was indeed a beautiful affair.

Jack attended Yale, earning a masters degree, an MPH. Fern was still a senior in college at Albany. I suggested that she complete her bachelor's degree in absentia at Yale. She did. At that time they lived in West Haven, Ct. Jack went on to attend Law

School at Rutgers University and Fern Alexander enrolled in a doctoral program at the University of Pennsylvania. They moved from West Haven and lived midway between both universities. They each earned their degrees.

The Eiferman Family, 1972 :
Irving, Jack, Leora, Deborah, and Loren

Less than ten years after they were married, Jack and Fern Alexander were divorced. Fortunately, they did not have any children. It was a relatively amicable break-up. Irv and I were devastated. We had learned to love our little, young daughter-in-law.

149

Sometime after Jack was divorced he met another person named Fern, Fern Fisher. She was a very different Fern. Physically she was tall, thin, dark haired and lovely. Fern Alexander was short, round, blond and pretty as well. The Ferns were not only physically different, but their personalities and demeanor differed as well. Since I had been in the field of personnel, I always said that if I had to interview possible candidates to marry our son and be a mother to our future grandchildren, Fern Fisher would get the position.

Jack and Fern Fisher wanted to get married at our home in Lake Waubeeka. We found a kosher caterer in New Haven who prepared a lovely meal. The wedding ceremony was outdoors in the back yard. It was conducted by our dear neighbor and friend, Rabbi Jerry Karlin. For the reception on the front lawn, we rented a tent with flaps in case of rain and heaters in case of cool temperature. Fortunately the weather was glorious. Bella Fisher, Fern's ebullient mother, wisely suggested we rent a dancing floor. The musicians and the dancing added much to the festivities. Bella was a dancing "pro". As part of the *simcha* (happy occasion), Jack and Fern planted a flowering, weeping apple tree which still graces our lawn, almost thirty years later. It was the holiday of *Lag B'Omer*. It was also Leora's 30th birthday, May 20, 1984. A double celebration!

I was concerned about the septic system in our

house accommodating about a hundred wedding guests. So we rented a Port-O-San as well. In addition to flowers at the center of each table, we placed some in the portable restroom, and hung some pictures. One of my friends, who had never used a portable facility, told me later on that it was so "accommodating, there was even a depression for a purse!" For those who also have never been in a portable facility, she was referring to the urinal!

Jack Eiferman and Fern Fisher, 1984

Sometime after the wedding, we had another reception for our friends whom we could not accommodate at the wedding. It was held in our lovely backyard in Connecticut under a circle of pine trees. The meal was cooked and catered by Debbie. I enjoyed the process. Jack and Fern enjoyed being at Lake Waubeeka so much they spent their honeymoon there. Irv and I graciously vacated the premises.

Over the years, we spent more time with Bella than with any of our other *machatanim* (in-laws) and got to know her more intimately. She visited with us in Lake Waubeeka and later on, frequently at Jack and Fern's home in Massachusetts. She was an outgoing, dynamic, attractive and independent woman. We also got to know Fern's affable brother Jeff. Fern's parents had been divorced some time ago. We met with her father, Bernie and his wife Claire, several times and liked them.

Ten months later Jack and Fern bestowed us with a miraculous gift, our first grandchild! Julia Fisher Eiferman. Jack kept us posted every step of the way. When we learned that Fern had left for the hospital, I insisted on immediately taking off from Lake Waubeeka for Boston. Irv, the more practical one, suggested that we wait until the baby was born. But there was no convincing this grandmother-to-be. We were on our way. We stopped at the first rest stop and called the hospital for the latest development. They informed us there was no "Fern Eiferman" currently registered as a patient. I began to worry. To be accurate, I began to panic. This was pre cell phones. We finally reached Boston, and went onto Storrow Drive and didn't know where to get off. This was pre-GPS as well. So we went round and round and round. After the third round, and finally with some accurate directions, we found the hospital. Fern Eiferman was not registered there, but Fern Fisher was! We met a proud daddy, a tired but glowing mommy and the most wonderful baby in the U.S, born on March 23, 1985. We were grandparents and Julia Fisher Eiferman was our stake in posterity! Her Hebrew name was *Yosephta*, after Irv's father.

About two and a half years later, on October 14, 1987, (it was also the holiday of *Hoshanah Rabbah*), the second miracle was born, Reva Fisher Eiferman. I never thought that the excitement and joy Julia generated could be duplicated. But here we were "ga-ga" over this new adorable wonder all over again. Reva was given the name of a cousin in Fern's family who was lost in the Holocaust.

Leora had been dating Tim Duch on and off for a number of years. Their relationship intensified. One evening Tim asked Irv for permission to marry our daughter. We could not say "no", they loved one another deeply. But it was a difficult and even a painful decision to make. We liked Tim, but he was not Jewish. We never imagined that any of our children would marry "outside the fold". We are observant Jews. We raised our children giving them a comprehensive Jewish education and assumed that their chosen spouses would be Jewish. It took a great deal of introspection to examine our feelings, decision and action. We raised our children to have a full grounding in Judaism. We also raised them to be autonomous adults. Therefore, it is incumbent upon us to respect their choices, even though they may differ from our expectations. So, with some apprehension we planned, with Leora and Tim's input, their wedding. We met Tim's parents and liked them very much. They had the very same reactions as we did, being devout Catholics. Aside from the difference of religion, I related to Pat Duch, Tim's mother, as a kindred soul. She was a warm, lovely and loving woman. Tim's father is a gracious gentleman.

Tim and Leora were married on February 23, 1986. The couple chose for their wedding ceremony, a place downtown Manhattan that had a view through lovely wrought iron grates. Leora wore an exquisite beaded dress a la the 1920's. A friend of ours, Judge Leon Deutch, performed the ceremony. The caterer we chose was Loren's former college roommate, Bavani, who is a gifted vegetarian caterer. The guests included our immediate families and close friends. The ambiance was just what Leora and Tim wanted. The food was delicious. It was good to meet and to become acquainted with Tim's brother and sisters for the first time.

Tim Duch and Leora Eiferman

Two years later, almost to the day, Leora gave birth, by cesarean section, to a beguiling baby boy, Nicholas Joseph Duch. He was named after Irv's father, Joseph. He was born February 14, 1988, on Valentine's Day and has been a child to love since the day he was born.

Loren was in no hurry to be born or to be married. At one time she was dating eight different guys. I asked her if she was interested in marrying any of them. She answered, "not at all". My response was, "tick tock, tick tock . . .". She got the "biological clock" message and told me, "When I meet the right person, I'll tell you. Don't worry."

Sometime later, I became aware that Loren was dating one person steadily. I asked her my usual question, "What is his last name?" She responded, that in time I will meet him. But she only said his name was "Joe". I kept nudging her and she finally said that his name was "Joe Berlinger". Berlinger was my maiden name! I told her I didn't have to meet him, I liked him already. Indeed, a discriminatory sentiment on my part.

We did arrange to get together in Lake Waubeeka for lunch. Irv barbequed salmon steaks as the main course. Unbeknownst to us, Joe disliked fish. He was a good sport, said nothing and decided to eat the meal. As Joe was picking up a piece of salmon on his fork everyone was in for a surprise. From the salmon perched on his fork, a thread-thin worm wiggled straight up! None of us had ever seen this sight before. Joe has not eaten salmon since, except for lox or gravad lax. Who could blame him?

One day our doorbell rang. It was our mailman, smiling broadly. He held up a postcard between his thumb and forefinger, waving it back and forth saying, "Mrs. Eiferman, you're gonna love this one!" And love it we did. It was a post card from Joe Berlinger addressed to Irving, asking for Loren's hand in marriage. He added on the card that even if Irv refused to grant his request "she already said yes." The card was posted on our refrigerator for ages and brought a smile to my face each time I glanced at it. I kept the card to this day.

It took some time and adjustment for us to learn

to develop "love" from "like" for each of our children's spouses. When parents are introduced to their child's choice for a life's partner, they tend to be apprehensive and cautious. It takes time to learn to appreciate each of the chosen one's special qualities and move beyond acquiescence to the partnership. It can be an enriching experience for a parent, when one realizes that the choice your child has made makes the child happy and fulfilled. Irv and I each had the *zechoot* (privilege) and good fortune to learn to truly love the new members of our family, chosen by our three children. We truly feel as if we have six loving children. They have not only enlarged the size of our family, they have enriched the Berlinger-Eiferman gene pool as well, adding music, math and height!

Three weddings and one more to go. It was Loren's turn. Motivated by innate curiosity, Joe's father and we checked our genealogical backgrounds and there was no connections between the Berlinger families for the past century. Whew! I'm not quite sure what the response would be if we were related. Now that I think of it, I do know. The marriage would take place anyway.

We invited Joe's parents to Waubeeka for a weekend, and later went with them to scout out a location for the upcoming nuptial. We did not find one. That was our only contact with Joe's parents prior to Joe and Loren's marriage. We delightedly met Joe's brother, Bob, the night before their wedding. For their wedding and reception a lovely Victorian mansion, Tarrywile, was rented. It had just been deeded to the city of Danbury and beautifully renovated and restored. Loren and Joe's wedding was one of the first ever held there. It was certainly the first kosher affair. The only disadvantage was that they (the fire department) would only allow 100 people in attendance. We were warned, 100 and one more, was a no-no. The date for the wedding was chosen, June 2, 1991.

Two months before, on April 13,1991, Fern gave birth to their son, Bennett Fisher Eiferman. He was named after Fern's father who had recently passed away. Little Bennett was the most popular person in our home at Lake Waubeeka. Aside from Jack and Fern, everyone vied to be with him, especially his three year old cousin, Nicky.

Loren wanted to be married under the lilac bush bower. Since the lilacs were no longer in full bloom they were married outdoors, along an arbor of blooming bushes. She looked lovely in a gown with layers and layers of tulle. Their *chupah* (canopy) was composed of four posts carved by Loren. It was draped in the embroidered shawl Bubby had brought with her when she came to America. Six year old Julia and four year old Reva were the adorable flower girls. Three year old Nicky was the ring bearer. In the middle of the ceremony he audibly informed the guests that a fly was caught in the tulle layers of Loren's gown!

We had a beautifully presented, catered, delicious *parve* meal. The mansion had a wrap around porch, as well as several lovely rooms including a dining room, a glass enclosed garden room and an enormous reception hall. The buffet was artfully presented in the dining room, the desserts were set in the garden room and there was dancing to the beat of a klezmer band in the reception hall. Tables were set on the porches and in various rooms. The day was beautiful, the wedding was spectacular, the couple magnificent and the band played on.

Loren Eiferman and Joe Berlinger

MEANDERING AND MOVING

From the time our children left for out of town college they never came to live back home. Apparently, that was the custom with most young people. Jack was married before he completed his graduate studies and lived in West Haven, Ct. Leora and Loren each moved to increasingly smaller, more expensive apartments, in areas that were awaiting gentrification, but were not there yet. As a result, they needed storage space for the items they didn't want to discard. So, as time went on, our large home accommodated their increasing collection of possessions as the numbers of our inhabitants decreased.

One of Leora's first apartments, prior to her marriage, was on the lower East Side. From her parents' point of view, this section of the city was probably the drug capital of the world. She told us that to ensure the protection of the tenants, the landlord had a steel door installed. Leora assured us that she was careful and cautious. She had her hair cut in a short bob. She wore a leather jacket, and at first glance, from a safety point of view, she looked like a boy. Of course there was a lovely empty bedroom for her in Brooklyn, but she would not have any of it. This is called the maturation process.

After they were married, Leora and Tim moved

to a loft in lower Manhattan, Hennington Hall, on East 2nd street near Avenue B. Coincidentally, it was the same building where Irv's *Bar Mitzvah* was held over 50 years earlier! From their pad in the lower East side they moved to the Cobble Hill section in Brooklyn. A far better choice, at least from a parent's perspective. It was great to have family back in Brooklyn, especially after grandchildren came along.

At the time, it was difficult to find an apartment with reasonable rent in Manhattan. (I know it is worse today). Loren, who was single at the time, heard of an empty apartment on Mulberry street in little Italy. She was interviewed by the landlord and assumed it was a done deal. She was contacted later the same day by the landlord and told that he was "sorry, but the apartment was not available". She was disappointed, and desperate to find an apartment. So, she decided to go back to the landlord and plead her case. She suspected that the refusal was motivated by something other than availability. So, she pleaded her case. When asked, she responded that her father was from Russia or Poland, but her mother was **Italian**. Later that day she got a call from the landlord that the apartment was hers! So ethnicity does play a role after all.

Somewhere around this time, Loren found or rather rescued, Anna, from a heap of garbage. She was a tiny, filthy, neglected and probably an abused kitten. Loren took her to a vet to get her cleaned,

161

inoculated and restored. Loren also got cleaned, a $400 bill! It was then that she asked herself, "what the heck did I do?" Anna remained her pet for many years. She was beyond anti-social to most, but she loved Loren.

The apartment that Loren was fortunate to get had much to be desired from my point of view. Where was the shower? Oh, there it is, a hose attached to the kitchen sink faucet. The toilet had an antique wooden water storage box, high above the seat in a tiny room, where is was difficult to even turn around. I wondered how a guy managed. Perhaps that's why the apartment was available to a female. The steps leading to the fifth floor were marble. No elevator. Each step had a deep, curved depression in the center, carved over the decades by multitudes of climbing feet. My heart sank when I visited her for the first and only time. But I have to admit it, she fashioned and decorated the place, maximizing its positives. Loren kept assuring us that it was a safe area. After all, it was in little Italy, the heart of the Mafia conclave.

After Loren and Joe were married they bought a co-op in Prospect Heights, Brooklyn. It was a former renovated public school, P.S. 9. The ceilings were 20 feet high. The windows had to be opened and closed with extended poles and a lot of effort. The towering room even had a loft. It was a relief to have her back in Brooklyn.

In the interim, Leora gave birth to a blue eyed, blond, adorable, baby boy, Jonah Evan Duch, on August 22, 1994. He enchanted his parents, brother and anyone who gazed at him. Leora and Tim were now cultivating two loving sons and a backyard "garden of Eden".

Six weeks later, October 17, 1994, Loren gave birth to a beautiful, blue eyed baby girl. She was named Sarah Amalia Berlinger, after Bubby. Gifts of joy were filling our treasury of love and posterity.

As time went on, thanks to our married children, we were blessed with wonderful grandchildren. I wanted to spend more time with them. Retire? Since Irv could be relatively flexible in his practice, I wanted to travel. Retirement would also enable me to spend more time pursuing sculpting in stone, a hobby that intrigues me.

Ner Tomid (Eternal Flame) Strawberry Alabaster

In 1986 I retired. For a number of semesters I stayed on at Brooklyn College as an adjunct professor, teaching one course, Psychosocial Development. For a few years after retiring, a colleague and I were also partners in a private counseling practice. Thus I enjoyed my gradual transition into retirement.

Deb and Irv, Brooklyn Botanic Garden.

THE BIG FIVE-O

1997.... I couldn't believe it. We were going to be celebrating our 50th wedding anniversary in December! The children said that they wanted to arrange a big party for us, celebrating the occasion. Giving it some considerable reflection, I came to an idea that excited both of us. We would not have the children host a party for us. Instead, we would take our whole family on a meaningful journey! We wanted the celebration to be something they would remember for the rest of "their" lives. Where to? Where else, but Israel. And so, I embarked upon a big project: planning a two week trip for fourteen individuals, ages ranging from three years old to 77 years young. Some basic guidelines served as the parameters for the venture. We would be together and still provide time and opportunity for each family to follow their predilection. So.... we would stay in the same hotels. We would try to aim to have at least one meal a day together. In towns, we would try to be centrally located. Jerusalem would be our base. Most of our touring "out of town" would be together.

The first problem was to get six adults to arrange "time off" from work for a two week period. There was some resistance, but I told them that everything had already been arranged, purchased and paid for and they didn't have much choice. After some juggling, all complied. We flew together on El Al leaving JFK at about midnight. Jack had arranged with El Al to have an anniversary cake with candles brought to us shortly after takeoff. We had a chorus of the planeload of passengers singing "Happy Anniversary" along with our family.

We rented four apartments, one for each family, in Jerusalem in *Lev Yerushalaim*, the heart of the city. It ended up that we had breakfast most days together. The children enjoyed the elevators, not having them at home. Whenever we were there, they moved around the hotel, up and down with joy and abandon. At the elaborate Israeli breakfasts, when we were usually together, we set the day's agenda. Each family went off on their own, following their individual interests. We usually met again together for dinner. In addition to touring the sites in Jerusalem and the Old City, we visited with friends who had made *aliyah* (emigrated to Israel). Fern, Jack and their children took off to visit with Fern's relatives who had settled in Israel. Since this was the first time Fern, Tim, Joe, Julia, Reva, Bennett, Nicky, Jonah and Sarah were in Israel there was much to see, visit and enjoy. We made a number of side trips to the Dead Sea, Haifa, Tel Aviv and up north. We visited our Halperin cousins at their kibbutz. They gathered their entire family to meet with us. It was a lovely, emotional get together. When we went touring in different parts of the country, we all traveled together. We rented a van, hired a driver and a guide. Our extra baggage was stored in *Lev Yerushalaim*. Some trips involved overnight or several night stays.

On one trip we went on a dig. The archeologist had the three year olds digging, screening and saving discovered shards which they could keep. The older children and the adults climbed down into the excavation by ladder. It was an exciting and educational experience. For my birthday a number of years ago, Nicky, as a gift, gave me a piece of pottery he had extracted at the dig and was told he could keep. He was nine years old at the time. Memories linger.

Another trip was to the Dead Sea where we had mud baths and some even sat on the water. Sarah was not happy there. She found the water too caustic. On another venture, the guide took the older children one evening to a shooting range, much to the consternation of some of us. We toured some of the churches and Christian sites as well. We also went to Masada. Irv and I met in the Zionist organization called "Masada", named after this place. It holds special significance for us. It was an amazing experience for me to revisit Masada.

In addition to the two three year olds, Jonah and Sarah, Bennett was six, Reva and Nicky were ten and nine, and Julia was almost 13. But there was a nascent addition as well! Loren was pregnant with our baby grandchild-to-be, Maya. The trip took place in December and extended into a few days of the new year. It was just about three months before the next family's celebration, Julia Fisher Eiferman's upcoming *Bat Mitzvah*.

1998 started out as a joyous year. We returned with the glow from our family trip to Israel, followed by the prospect of Julia's *Bat Mitzvah* in March. It was a wonderful, happy occasion. Julia "did us proud". Jack and Fern successfully hosted their first lovely family affair. Our entire family was there, my sisters and their families. Relatives came from California, from Florida and Cousin Ruth from Washington, D.C. It was so wonderful to have all the people we love together. In the years following, Julia's siblings and cousins also brought us *nachas* (pride and joy) as they participated in their *Bar and Bat* Mitzvahs with confidence and competence.

One can only anticipate the future, but not foretell it. One morning, as Irv was dressing, I noticed that his little toe was red and swollen. And so began a new chapter in our lives.

THE LITTLE RED MENACE

Stemming from a seemingly insignificant fact, the red swollen little toe on his foot, our lives were turned around. It looked "angry" to me. Irv poo-pooed it and said it was nothing. It had been a blister and really didn't bother him. But the next day I marched him over to the podiatrist's office. He took a culture, said it looked like a staph infection and Irv should take an antibiotic (penicillin), just in case. We followed instructions. After two doses of the antibiotic Irv was covered from head to toe with a red, chenille-like rash. We went to a doctor's office two blocks away. He diagnosed the condition as Stevens Johnson syndrome, a potentially fatal reaction, if not caught in time. Irv was advised "never, never take penicillin again". The biopsy result came back and it was indeed a staph aureus infection. No other antibiotic was prescribed. The toe apparently healed. But, did it?

Some time later Irv collapsed in the bathroom. Hatzalah, a volunteer ambulance service, was called. He was rushed to the emergency room at Long Island College Hospital in downtown Brooklyn. After a series of testing and imaging, I was told that he had a growth on his spine. He needed emergency surgery which was being scheduled for the next morning. My wonderful support system, our three children, went into three alarm mode. In consultation with computer validation and our dear friend from Lake Waubeeka, Dr. Moe Nussbaum, we were referred to a skilled back surgeon at Beth Israel Hospital, Dr. Paul Kuflick. A transfer to Beth Israel Hospital, diagnosis and subsequent surgery took place within days. Indeed he had a benign tumor on his lower spine. It was a staph aureus infected tumor. Subsequent recovery and rehabilitation took place at the Hospital for Joint Disease. The hospitals were around the corner from each other, yet an ambulance had to be used for the transfer. We could have wheeled him there in less time, effort and expense. But, we are mandated to abide by established regulations. Initially there was a question of whether Irv could walk again. With the good work of the hospital's rehabilitation staff and Irv's determination, he was discharged, walking and wearing a back brace.

While Irv was in the hospital, my knee gave out and I could barely walk. The doctor arranged immediate out-patient arthroscopic knee surgery. My poor kids had a difficult time with both parents hospitalized and incapacitated. Leora and Tim took me into their home for post operative recovery. The recovery was more painful than the procedure. We rented an ice machine to ease the pain. They were gracious and caring. The grandchildren were delightful diversions.

Upon discharge from the hospital, Irv resumed his practice, at first on a limited basis. Within a short time he was back to his daily routine. There he was, litigating in court every Monday through Thursday. He thrived.

In the meantime Loren gave birth to our baby granddaughter, Maya Rebekah on September 12, 1998, the same day and month as her uncle Jack. Her birth represented another *simcha* (happy occasion) in our family thanks to Loren and Joe. It was hard to believe that another sibling could match adorable, bright Sarah. But Maya did and continues to do so in her own inimitable way. After the birth of Maya, we were informed that the grandchildren shops were closed. What a great *nachas* bundle we already had.

A year later, almost to the date, Irv collapsed again. He was rushed to Beth Israel Hospital and the same routine was followed. Another infected growth on his spine, benign, staph aureus was found and surgically removed. This time he didn't bounce back.

He had a series of additional imaging and medical consultations. We were told that he would have to undergo one or more surgeries. I asked the doctor what Irv's prognosis was. He replied that there was none. However, he could give me a prognosis if Irv did not forgo the recommended surgery. Death. I went home and cried and cried some more. Was this the end? At the moment when I realized that this was just about hopeless, I literally realized that things could not get worse. **But**, things could only get better. "Flip the coin around Debbie. Pray, miracles happen. He may very well survive. Hope and pray."

Around the same time Loren was explaining to Sarah that Poppa was in the hospital and was very sick. Three year old Sarah's response was, "Let us pray". Surprised, Loren wondered what Sarah was being taught in nursery school. "Where did you learn about praying?" To which Sarah responded, "Mommy, don't you remember when we were in Israel, in Jerusalem, at a big wall with holes in it. You told me we can wish and pray for something we want to happen very much and we can write the wish down on paper and put it in a hole in this wall. Well, we aren't at that wall but we can pray for something we wish very much. We can pray for Poppa."

To shorten and summarize, Irv was in the ICU for over thirty days, had five surgeries under general anesthesia in a six week period. We were advised that since he had so many surgeries under general anesthesia, within so short a time, his memory may be effected. He remained in the hospital for 100 days. How come and why? When he was unable to walk this time, the doctor ordered a complete imaging from head to toe. They discovered, in layman's terms, that the staph infection "ate up" a good deal of his spine. So, with the miracle of the doctors' skill and current medical knowledge, they scraped and cleaned the infected bone and installed two steel bars to stabilize his spine. To further stabilize his spine, a titanium cage was inserted between his damaged vertebrae. I was now married to a bionic miracle!

The "why" was not answered until they discovered that his little toe was the feeding site. They operated and removed the source of the infection. It was a medical mystery solved. Next he embarked on a miraculous medical recovery. That was my Irving, persistent, stubborn and determined!

REASSURING RECOVERY

When I recall aspects of that period, they are interspersed with some humor and memorable interludes. For example: frequently, the psychiatrist on staff, who was assigned to Irving, would come by and ask him what was today's date. Imagine being hospitalized, living in an alien world among the society of the ill, and knowing today's date! Or he would ask who the President was. Once, when I was present at this interrogation, this was Irv's response: "Dr., if you don't know who the current President is, perhaps you should take a hiatus in your medical practice and go back to school, or at least take time out to read a daily newspaper." That was my lawyer lover's response.

I found it very difficult to deal with problems arising in his hospital stays, from seeking information regarding his progress, to requesting changes, to finding out about transfers being made without informing us. When we had to get satisfaction I turned to my support trio, my children, to do it. They did. But one day Loren told me, "Mom, you have to learn to be a bitch." My nature is such that I am usually not aggressive. Loren wanted me to be definitively more assertive. I told her it was difficult for me to change my modus operandi. I did however, agree to be "a bitch in training", so I assiduously practiced being a "**BIT**".

The children, Jack, Leora and Loren, were an ongoing support system. They visited frequently and participated in every decision that had to be made. Jack lived in Massachusetts and either drove in or flew frequently to visit and consult.

Irv must have had an unusual tolerance for pain. He rarely complained of having any. Once in a while, when it was obvious that he was experiencing discomfort, he would nod in the affirmative. At the time that he was in the ICU, they had just installed a relatively new devise, a pain pump. The patient could press a button whenever he or she was in pain and a measured dose of medication would be administered. After several days the nursing staff removed his pain pump. Why? Because he never used it.

In the hospital each patient was assigned a physician to serve as a coordinator among the various disciplines involved with the patient. I was having difficulty finding out from the six, yes, I said six, different physicians in six different disciplines, what the score was with Irving. The coordinating doctor was never available. Apparently the five other doctors were having difficulty hearing from him as well. I checked with the administration and Dr. Nussbaum and was advised that no change could be made unless he was reassigned or he was fired. The coordinating physician would not be reassigned.

One morning when I was at Irv's bedside THE DOCTOR marched in, glanced at Irv's chart, asked him how he was "do'n" and started to leave. I called out to him, asked him who he was. (I'll call him Dr. Jones.) "Oh", I said, " you are the famous Dr. Jones. You may be a very good physician, but you are no longer Irving Eiferman's doctor. Good bye." He blanched, looked shocked. I reiterated that we did not want him to be Irv's doctor any longer. I fired him. I was learning to be a BIT!

Dr. Nussbaum, at our request, then recommended Dr. Sidney Stein to serve as the coordinating physician. Dr. Stein agreed. He was and is excellent. He continued to care for both of us. Dr. Nussbaum was instrumental in many ways, from the choice of doctors, to his being personally present in the operating room during each of Irv's five surgeries. I attribute Irv's survival, to large extent, to Dr. Nussbaum's interventions and efforts. He is no longer with us. He was an amazing, caring and skillful human being. We miss him.

Six doctors said that Irv would never walk again. In layman's terms, we were advised that despite the fact that the muscles of his legs were intact and strong, the nerves were injured. He could and would not walk again. Irv responded by saying they were crazy, he was going to walk again. The long road of rehabilitation and recovery began.

REHABILATATION

From Beth Israel Hospital Irv was transferred to the "spinal injury unit" at Mount Sinai Hospital in upper Manhattan. It was an excellent rehabilitation unit. They worked with Irv. His determination and progress motivated the physical and occupational therapy staff. In his usual outgoing manner, Irv got to know and interact with his fellow patients. He remained there for several months. When it came time to discharge him from a hospital "rehab" facility to an outpatient rehabilitation establishment, I went into exploring mode. I visited several centers. It was important to Irv to be in a kosher place, or at least where kosher food was an option. The locations ranged from New Jersey, the Bronx, Manhattan to Brooklyn. I spent time in each, interviewed and observed the physical therapy staff as well as assessed the setting, program and facilities. We finally settled on the Shorefront in Brooklyn. I was impressed with their physical therapy set-up, staff, kosher kitchen and beautiful location. It turned out to be an ideal location for me to visit. It was on the Boardwalk in Coney Island.

Let me digress and tell you why. I was never motivated to drive. Irv walked to work everyday and the car was always in the driveway. So when

Jackie was an infant, I decided that I should learn to drive. I took lessons. Both Irv and I realized that in order to practice for the test, after one disastrous try, it would be best if he would **not** be my instructor. I seem to recall going out with my brother-in-law, David, to practice driving. After two tries I passed the driving test. As soon as I received my license in the mail suddenly the car was no longer in its usual spot! For some reason, Irv was using it every day. I got the message. I accepted the status quo since I was honestly never motivated to be a driver. However, years later, when we would not permit Irv to drive, I realized that I had to take the wheel. We still commuted to Lake Waubeeka when Irv was recovering. We had to hire a driver. I realized that unless I could drive we would have to sell our vacation home. We didn't want to do that. So, I eventually relearned to drive and began driving in earnest. More on this later on.

When Irv was in the hospitals for months, I initially traveled by subway on my daily visits. However, since I went every morning and returned at night, travel was a burden. I decided to treat myself and took car service. On rare mornings, during the summer, I took the *Bikur Cholim* bus. It was a volunteer transportation service run by a Jewish non profit organization. *Bikur Cholim* means "visiting the sick". The van did several pick ups in Brooklyn and also picked up *glatt kosher* meals for patients in several Manhattan hospitals. Women volunteers took the food to the hospital patients. These patients preferred food which was prepared under strict, kosher dietary conditions. It was an interesting trek around Brooklyn neighborhoods and stops at four or five Manhattan hospitals. It took over two hours to reach my destination.

I visited with Irving every day, arriving late morning and leaving around eight o'clock in the evening. The car service was waiting for me. It made my transportation manageable. Beth Israel Hospital was at 2nd avenue and 16th street and Mount Sinai was at 122nd street, all some distance from our home in Brooklyn.

The Shorefront Rehab center faced the Atlantic Ocean and the Boardwalk. Daily, I gladly drove the car there. Irv was happy in that setting. When Irv was hospitalized, we had Passover *sedorim* at his bedside. Beth Israel had a kosher kitchen and supplied the *seder* fixings. We spent the High Holidays at the Shorefront at their patient synagogue. Overnight stays were arranged for me during the holidays. I slept on a cot in Irv's room and found myself ambivalently grateful he was alive, but unhappy in the setting and circumstances.

HOME AT LAST

When Irv was ready to be discharged, he was confined to a wheel chair. Realizing that the six step entrance to our home was a problem, I arranged for a carpenter to build a ramp in front of the house. He figured how much lumber was needed. The lumber was delivered the week before the homecoming. I then shared the plan with Irv. He was infuriated! He declared he was going to walk and there was no need for a ramp. He made it very clear that no ramp was to be built.

Before I had a chance to cancel the ramp, I got a call from the carpenter that he was unable to do the job for another few weeks. Irv informed the occupational therapist at Shorefront that he had to learn to climb steps before he was discharged! He learned the mechanics but he still needed assistance. When he came home, Jackie carried his father into the house.

I realized that I was unable to push Irv in the wheelchair. My shoulders weren't up to the push. Despite his efforts and progress, I was also concerned about my ability to support Irv when he was transferring to and from the wheel chair. I decided to hire help. Irv made it clear that he did not want a woman hired, only a man.

I contacted a local agency. Most clients wanted a woman. I interviewed the young man who happened to be available. In addition to the referral by the agency, I think that he must have been sent to us by heaven! He came from the country of Georgia. He could speak English, but it could use some brushing up. In Georgia he ran a nursing agency. He was a graduate of a Russian medical school. I learned that he had come to the U.S. to qualify to practice medicine as a plastic surgeon. He could work for us "almost" full time. He needed to leave late in the day to go to Kaplan's to brush up on his English and prepare for his Medical Boards. His name was Khakha. I was impressed by this young man. I detailed his responsibilities. I also explained that we were orthodox, to orient him to kosher dietary laws, since he would be living with us. When he heard "orthodox", he brightened and said with a smile. "I too, Orthodox". I realized he meant Russian Orthodox! He would have a room, closet and storage space in a bedroom on the second floor. But we expected him to sleep on the first floor within earshot of Irving. In addition to his professional skills he was "tall, dark and handsome". It was serendipity. He was a gift. His nature was gracious. He was intelligent, knowledgeable, meticulous and a delight to have live with us. With Khakha we had a built in doctor, nurse, physical therapist, care giver and friend. We

181

arranged to accommodate his school schedule and hired a Russian man to come in the evenings to put Irv to sleep.

We changed the front room, the library, into Irv's bedroom and rented a hospital bed and commode. Tim built a lovely silk screen to give Irv privacy. The major disadvantage was that we had no full bath on the first floor. Khakha sponge bathed and messaged Irv every day. There was a half wall separating the open living room from the adjacent dining room. Khakha slept on a cot next to the half wall. It gave him some privacy and yet he was near Irving. He opened and folded the cot every day. As he cared for Irv, there was some reciprocity. Irv helped him in brushing up his English. He also taught Irv some Russian words. He was a superb gift. We had originally hired him for about two months. He lived with us for almost a year and became a dear member of our household. I'm not sure how I would have coped without him.

Once Irv came home, the white squares on our calendar were rapidly filled in with appointments with doctors and physical therapists and for transportation pickups and returns. We even arranged to spend some brief visits to Waubeeka. Khakha drove. It was a busy time.

NEXT STEPS

Irv steadily progressed, graduating from the wheel chair to a walker and finally to a four pronged cane. He resumed his energetic walking routine with relish and vigor.

For a while we lived in our home in Connecticut during the Spring, Summer and Fall. Irv needed outpatient infusions periodically for a bladder infection. In New York, outpatient infusions were limited to cancer patients. The infusions in New York would only be administered to Irving on a hospital inpatient basis. We were able to arrange for the outpatient procedures at Danbury Hospital. I did not drive. As I mentioned before we realized that unless I learned to drive, we would have to give up our home in Connecticut. So, learn I did.

Thirty some odd years ago I had a driver's license but never drove. We hired the unemployed husband of Irv's aide in Connecticut to teach me. I was particularly concerned about highway driving. He took me out several mornings a week, learning and practicing driving in the local Danbury Mall parking lot and later on the highways. So at seventy-five years old I began solo driving.

Our home in Brooklyn had two stories and a basement, where the washing machine and dryer were located. Living there became more inconvenient as time went on. With the vigorous urgings of our three children, we began to explore where our next home would be. Jackie opted for Brookline Massachusetts. We looked at some apartments there. Although, in addition to Jack and Fern and their family and Brookline being a "senior friendly" and culturally desirable community, we rejected that choice. It meant that we would be too far from Lake Waubeeka, as well as some of the benefits we loved about living in New York City. At the suggestion of our friend in Lake Waubeeka, Jeannie Kaufman, I subscribed to the Riverdale Press. We learned that the community in Riverdale offered all, and more, of the positives we had in Brooklyn, and still an easy commuting distance to the city and to Connecticut. I assiduously embarked on an apartment hunting project in Riverdale. Irv had been confined to a wheelchair for about a year, although by this point he no longer was. I therefore looked for a building that had no entrance steps and had access to the elevators and mailroom without steps. That combination was not easy to find. Over a period of several months I saw thirty two apartments and finally settled on one. Did I say "one"? No, it was two apartments. The prior owner combined two apartments, resulting in more closet space and a double terrace. It was the view that precipitated my final choice. It was breathtaking.

From every window we behold the panorama of the Palisades, the Hudson River and the sky. Once we moved in, we never pull our window shades down. Sunsets are spectacular and we reserve that time to just sit, savor and appreciate the ever-changing splendor.

We sold our home in Brooklyn in three days. It was during the real estate bubble. The bubble was not at its height nor did it burst, but it was bubbling. The wife of the couple who bought our home never looked at it. They knocked the house down and planned to rebuild. They were only interested in the location.

All my life I had lived in private homes. I am not an elitist, but I was very apprehensive about living in a multiple dwelling. I was in for pleasant surprises. The doormen announce guests, accept packages, help to unload the car and take messages. The efficient, gracious staff change light bulbs and is always available for minor repairs. The garbage disposal is down the hall. No snow to shovel! Shortly after we moved in there was a heavy snowfall. I went out onto the terrace and starting sweeping. When Irv asked, "What in the world are you doing?" I replied, "I'm getting withdrawal symptoms!"

RIVERDALE

We loved living in Riverdale. I still do. It is a cohesive, friendly community, abounding in cultural activities. We developed friendships with a number of bright, supportive, wonderful, younger friends. Many of our activities involved our synagogue, the Conservative Synagogue Adath Israel of Riverdale, which we joined. We also joined the "Y". To Irv's delight, the public library is within easy walking distance, only a block and a half away from our building. He was a daily visitor. Now that he was able to walk, assisted only with a quad cane, he took frequent walks around the block and to the library. That is, until he tripped several times. He was not hurt, but his solo strolls were now restricted. He always asked me to go with him. Not being a walker, I usually didn't meet his requests. Yet, the challenge was to let him tread that thin line between "dependence" and "independence".

Although Irv had some limitations regarding his ability to carry out daily living activities, he never complained. He was unable to bend. He had two steel bars stabilizing his spine as well as a titanium cage between two vertebrae. As I said, I called him "my bionic miracle". He never complained to me. His attitude was positive. He sometimes commented to his doctors about his frustration regarding diminishing physical ability as well as his short term memory. It was important for me to try to insure that we didn't compromise his sense of self respect and self esteem. Rarely did he become verbally assertive. It was always only in front of our children. Perhaps it was his way of showing them that he was still head of the family.

For about ten years Irv had "MCI", mild cognitive impairment. It was manifested in a number of ways. He repeated the same questions, we no longer had deep discussions about material he had read and he tended to enjoy the same programs over and over again. He also had difficulty remembering names, but so do many older adults. I do not think that he had Alzheimer's Disease, since although his memory declined somewhat over the ten year period, it did not decline precipitously. Perhaps the medications he was taking served as holding actions. He did not display other symptoms of AD. He continued to read books, but not at the former pace. I am not sure how much of the material he retained. I missed our discussions. He continued to be outgoing and amiable. Irv always told me how grateful he was for our having each other. His expressions of love and gratitude were never by rote, but rather in various circumstances and many times during the day and night too. Although I missed some aspects of our life before he became ill, I was content.

During this period we continued to commute to Lake Waubeeka, spending more time there during the summer months and periodic visits the rest of the year. When I started writing this opus, I related a vignette of my Bubby Runya amusing me in the attic in Borough Park. She would twirl her diamond heart locket in the sunshine, producing a whirling carousel of rainbows. As she watched my utter delight, she always said that someday, I would have the locket. The coda follows: Upon Bubby's death my aunt Ida inherited her mother's jewelry. Cousin Helen and finally cousin Ruth, were next in line when their mother, aunt Ida, died. When Ruth passed away in Washington D.C., there was an estate sale of her possessions. My children learned of the sale and arranged to buy one of the items. You guessed which one. For my 80th or 85th birthday, we had a "gathering of the clan" in Lake Waubeeka. My children, to my surprise, presented the diamond studded heart to me. I was overwhelmed with love, appreciation and treasure filled memories.

SISTERS

Although this is the last chapter I am writing, it is being inserted into the approximate correct chronological sequence. Why the last? Because, for me, it probably has been one of the most difficult. So, I kept putting off the writing. The death of my mother, father, Jerry and Irving were so hard to re-live. The death of my sisters represented the last living connection to my early history and beyond. When the cord was severed, my original nuclear family was gone.

As far back as I can remember, my two sisters and I had a very close, loving relationship. Perhaps it may have been impelled and strengthened by the death of my mother when we were so young. We depended on, supported and confided in each other as we were growing up and later when we were older. Although in recent decades, we were geographically separated, Evie lived in Florida, Ronnie in Amherst, Massachusetts and we lived in New York, our phone contact with each other was frequent. No texting or e-mails, just long, intimate, phone connections. In addition to our Sisters Week, Passover and Thanksgiving were other time that the three of us were together. We spent long, glorious weekends, along with the whole family, for many years, at the Grist Mill in Amherst at Ronnie and Hill's home. Other years we would take a trip or two to visit each other.

Since my sister Ronya was only six years old when our mother passed away, her vulnerability, was an impetus for maternal feelings in me. She was an adorable child, developed into a winsome adolescent, a bright student, and then into a loving wife and mother. In addition, she was gifted, very bright and creative. She possessed many other positive characteristics, bearing them with grace, intelligence and inner beauty.

She developed lung cancer. Shortly after her 71st birthday, she passed away in the hospice in Amherst on April 14, 2004. I did get to be with her, all too briefly.

Evelyn was three years younger than me. We went through the same stages and experiences in tandem. Evie was my role model, my confidant, my sage advisor and consultant. She was bright, organized, efficient, practical, generous, loving and the sweetest person I ever encountered. She developed cell b carcinoma and kidney cancer. The day before her 82nd birthday, on December 27, 2007, she passed away in hospice. Once again, I only reached a beloved sister just before her dying day. Both of them were younger than me and I mourn them. It is something I never thought or expected to happen. I continue to miss them.

GROWTH

"Growth". The word to me has always involved a positive element, sometimes "forward movement", other times "directional improvement". Now suddenly it has a sinister connotation.

The doctor gave us the diagnosis and referred to a "mass" or a "growth". The words not only impinged physically but also insinuated themselves into our psyche. Something not seen and, thankfully, not yet felt, had become a major factor in our lives. The parameters of life have limits – nothing is forever. But when one realizes the finality, no matter when, it upsets composure. We had much to learn in order to accommodate the effect it would have on our lives. Following "shock", "regret" and "sadness" was" acceptance" of the inevitable and an attempt to smooth the transition.

We were told that Irv had a large "growth", an inoperable cancer, in his bladder. We hoped and tried to savor the precious time we had left.

SHALOM

As had been our custom for the past decade or so, we enjoyed part of Passover at Jack and Fern's home. The *sedorim* are beautiful. Each year they update, revise and enhance the *Hagadah*, adding significant elements while retaining the traditional sections. Each guest reads portions of the service. Jack and Fern jointly conduct the *sedar*. When they reach *Hallel*, Irv usually takes over. This year when Jack turned to Irv, Irv nodded his head, declining. It was the first time he ever refused. Whereupon the grandchildren took over and started chanting the *Hallel*, as if on cue. It was a transformative moment for me.

Several days later during *chol hamoed Pesach* (the middle days of the Passover holiday), when we were preparing to go home, back to Riverdale, Irv suddenly became very weak. Our reliable driver, Roger, practically carried Irv into the car. I called Dr. Stein. We saw him in his office the next morning. From there he was rushed to Beth Israel Hospital by ambulance. In order to avoid the emergency room he was admitted to the VIP unit. As sick as he was, Irv wanted to know if the food was kosher for Passover! It was.

When I returned to the hospital the next morning there were two of our grandsons on either side of Irving, holding his hands. Nicky had left work at Tishman and Bennett had left classes at NYU to be with their "Poppa"! It was a heart- rending scene. The rest of the family came later on. Irv's condition was declining. After two days, the medical decision was to transfer him to the hospice floor. He needed pain relief. I was asked to sign the admission forms. The thought that assaulted my mind was " I'm signing his death warrant!". I know the transfer was a valid medical decision, to make him more comfortable, but I couldn't shake my reluctant acceptance of the inevitable.

While visiting Irv on the hospice floor, members of the family sometimes wandered into the library, a few doors away from Irv's room. One evening Loren glanced at a bookshelf in the library and saw a volume that interested her, the _Zohar_. As she later told us, she thought at the time: "I'm past 50, so I'm old enough to read it". She randomly opened it to chapter 18. It was entitled "Where Do We Go After We Die?" and the next words she read were: "What happens when Israel is gone?" She flipped out. Irv's Hebrew name was _Yisrael_!

Rabbi Katz, our Rabbi, visited Irving. At the next visit, he told us that he thought that the end was near. The family convened. It was hard for me then to believe that in so short a time, how many family members managed to get together. Our children, their spouses, our grandchildren, our niece, Freda and grandnephew, David and even a family member-to-be came. In the past, it would be by phone or telegram and today it's by text or tweet. What brought everyone here? Surely, the gravity of the situation, but additionally, the strands of love and respect tugged at each one.

Irving was medicated to minimize the pain. He was not alert. However the nurse once again assured us that he was able to hear. Rabbi Katz facilitated the *veedui*, the special prayer for the end of life. Rabbi Katz and the family surrounded his bed. Since he was heavily medicated, Irv was not able to actively participate. We therefore all chanted the prayer in unison on Irving's behalf. It was an emotional tribute to him and to our wonderful family.

Although Irv did not appear conscious, as I said, we were told by the hospice staff that the last sense to go was hearing. She encouraged us to speak to him individually and not about him. Each of us took our turn, one by one and spoke to him. Some whispered into his ear; others talked to him about what was on and in their minds and hearts. Each one was accorded the appropriate privacy. In discussion later, one said that she wished him well on his journey to the unknown. Another found it hard to let him go. One asked forgiveness for a forgotten misdeed. Several said they just expressed their love for him. Others recalled cherished memories. Each one enclosed their *shalom* (goodbye) to him in an envelop of love.

Although there was no question that death was hovering in that hospice room, so was there love and an overwhelming life force permeating the ambience.

From the time he was admitted to hospice, palliative care was the modus operandi. He was heavily sedated and tended to be semi conscious. I sat at his bedside listening to his syncopated, open mouthed, rasping breath. What was going through my mind was, "why": Is my beloved husband fighting to stay alive, or is dying such a struggle? Yet, there he was lying in bed, unmoving, inert except for his labored breathing. It was a heart-breaking enigma followed by a wrenching dilemma. Do I keep praying to keep him alive or do I reluctantly let him go? Yet, despite these fervent introspections, I knew in my heart of hearts that it isn't, and never was, up to me.

Irv died on April 12, 2012 at 9:55P.M. surrounded by the people he loved and who loved him. He was 92 years old.

SHIVA

It was a busy week. Many visitors, family, including my nephew, Michael, from California and my niece, Julie from Mass., my niece Freda, my friends and my children's friends from near and far, neighbors, and even people we hardly knew came to express their condolences. It was in part a foggy experience. It is called the week of *Shiva*, meaning seven. It stands for the seven days of mourning following the burial of an immediate family member.

It is a traditional and helpful practice within Judaism. For me it was also a week of psychological exploration, healing and acceptance. It also served as the beginning of the transitional time adjusting to my new role. Although I found the week physically tiring, other aspects were psychologically helpful in the mourning process. They included a deep appreciation of having my supportive, loving children with me 24/7, accessing memories which were not forgotten after all, resolving some issues and re-uniting with friends of long standing, be it by person or pen.

At the end of the *Shiva* period, when my daughter, Leora and I took the traditional walk around the block together, I was overcome with an odd dual feeling. A feeling of ending, which is to be expected, but also a feeling of beginning.

MOURNING IN THE MORNING

I awaken in the morning, as usual at 5:30 AM, not by a clock, just by my inner alarm clock. I don't get out of bed. I look at the clock radio every half hour or so. I try to guess the time. I'm pretty good at it, usually no more than 10 or 15 minutes off. I consider that a relatively good inner clock. I realize I have no appointments for the day, go back to sleep, reawaken at 7 , fall asleep again and finally get up and out of bed at 9. Now what? A blank schedule. No appointments with doctors or therapists. No transportation "pick up and return" times.

I go to the bathroom and as I am brushing my teeth, I glance at the medicine chest mirror above the sink. Realizing I am in a negative slump, I think: "You lost your job Deborah. What now?" I feel as if I reached bottom. "I have nowhere to go. Or do I? How about up? Flip the coin, just as you did 14 years ago, when Irv was hospitalized". As crazy as it was, I smiled! Then and there I decided to try to seek a more positive frame of mind. I admit, there are times I feel silly, smiling when I feel so rotten. Just looking at my vacuous, incongruous, forced, smiling reflection is enough. Perhaps this ridiculous action on my part can be a catalyst for wiping away the negativity I experience.

Irving and I were married for 64 inspiring years. I miss him terribly, morning, noon and especially at night. I began to express my grief concretely. Each morning, after my medicine chest smile, as a reminder, I vent my heartache via poetry. I had penned some poetry on occasion, years before. I found writing about how I felt to be a source of solace and comfort.

One day, as I was going through some papers, I found an announcement in an AARP publication about a poetry contest sponsored by *Passager*, a magazine devoted to publishing works by seniors. I submitted. I had never done that before. I won an honorable mention and one of my poems, "Remnants", was published! What an ego trip that was!

REMNANTS

His fingerprints inside the mirrored door of
the medicine chest
I'll wipe it down another time.
His smell, no, his aroma on his pillowcase
I'll wash it another time.
A silver hair entwined in the bristles of his
boar's hair brush
I'll unwind it another time.

He's not here

He is where?
There?
Everywhere?
Anywhere?

I'll seek another time.

2013

TRANSCENDENT TIMES

Most of this opus has focused on my memories of family and personal events. I realize that a glaring omission is the impact of world events on my life. I have lived through an amazing transcendent period. The times ranged from terrible, to transmuting, to transforming, to triumphant, not necessarily in that order. I will briefly enumerate the arc of this phenomenal era in which I have lived.

I was born during the "Roaring Twenties" in 1923, a period characterized, in part, by post World War I economic prosperity, Art Deco, patriotism and jazz. The "flapper" exemplified the modern woman. It was part of the beginning of feminism. Perhaps that is why the headline in the newspaper when I was born was "women will rule this year". As an aside, over 90 years later, we still haven't achieved that goal yet.

I do not remember anything about "the crash" of 1929. Our family was comfortable until the depression of the 1930's . I wrote about living and growing up during that period. Since my father was in the high end jewelry business he apparently was able to support the family economically by designing unique items and repairing jewelry.

In the late 1930's, as a teenager, I became aware of the tragic circumstances of the Jewish people in Europe. I was active, along with a group of my peers, in protesting. We marched and wrote letters in the hope that the United States would take a more active role to help the refugees and use its influence to stop the horrible, inhuman exterminations.

Once we entered World War II, our activities increased. There were many programs to support the war effort, some government sponsored, and others voluntary, e.g., rationing, war bond sales, blood drives. We were personally involved in the war in some way on a daily basis. Many of our peers and family were in the service overseas which further motivated our participation.

As information about the holocaust trickled out, the horror assaulted belief in humanity. We felt incapacitated and our only hope was lodged in the outcome of the war. Our individual support and participation in the war effort intensified. So many of our young contributed, not money, not only blood, but with their lives.

During the post war years the economy rebounded. Some of the national events and facts that stay in my mind (not in chronological order or importance) include: the death of President Roosevelt, the WPA (Works Progress Administration), Eleanor Roosevelt's role in the UN passing the Declaration of Human Rights, passing the Social Security Act, the assassinations of President Kennedy, Robert Kennedy and Martin Luther King in succession, the passing of the Civil Rights Act, the long years of the Bushes, Clinton's administration, the beginning move to address climate change, and currently the first black U.S. President, Barak Obama. I am still waiting to have a woman President in my lifetime.

Perhaps for me the most exciting political, event was the UN vote that established the State of Israel. Irv and I sat at our table, pad and pencil in hand, recording the UN count as the votes were announced over the radio. It was the culmination of a dream come true. I think that was the happiest, diplomatic, legislative miracle I ever experienced.

My life has spanned a multifaceted range of national and world events from tragic to inspirational. I gratefully have had the privilege to live during momentous, fluid periods.

PERSPECTIVES

I have written basically a series of memories from my past, my autobiography or a memoir. I want to note that I deliberately did not focus individually on the dearest members of my family; not on my children, Jack, Leora or Loren and not on their spouses, Fern, Tim or Joe. Why? They are all special to me. They have been, and are, a source of pleasure and *nachas*. Writing about them would delimit, earmark, curb and delineate. For me they are current, vital and ongoing. Therefore I only included snippets of some experiences, as I remember them.

How could I even forget to write about my grandchildren, as I call them, my "stakes in posterity"? There too, I didn't want to freeze them in time. They are evolving, maturing, developing, blossoming, flourishing and thriving. I found that I couldn't focus on so many special moments of my cynosures, my amazing, unique, bright, loved, special seven:

Julia, Bennett, and Reva Fisher Eiferman, 2013

Nicholas Joseph and Jonah Evan Duch

Maya Rebekkah and Sarah Amalia Berlinger

This opus is basically finished. Why is it that for the past month or so, I have once again avoided reaching this point? Perhaps, because as I wrote and dredged up what I thought were "should have been forgotten" memories, I psychologically re-lived them. Some were painful, but only some. As I wrote, I was focusing on the past. According to Paul Valery in <u>Cahiers</u> "Memory is the future of the past". Yet, in my head and where I am, when I am not writing, I am infused with the "here and now".

One of my idiosyncrasies is to look for and find acronyms. So why not with the word "now"? How about Noting Ongoing Wonder, or better yet, Nourishing Ongoing Wonder? There is something very special about "now". The present is something everyone experiences and is here, current, never to be repeated. I try to make the most of it. It is encompassing and can be fulfilling. Even if the present, "now", is terrible and /or painful, shortly, it will be gone. It, i.e. "now", will be over. If it is good, peaceful, eventful or even uneventful, I am aware and live in the moment.

For the past decade or so, Irv and I had a morning ritual. Before we got out of bed, we recited the *shehecheeyahnu* (a Hebrew prayer of gratitude). We then listed in detail, each entity on our present gratitude list. I still mourn that morning ritual.

Our lives are shaped and nuanced by experiences and events over which we rarely anticipate or can control. Aside from missing Irv, and I don't put that phrase in as an automatic preamble, but rather to place my current circumstances and ideas into a more realistic and honest perspective, I am content at this stage of my life. It's more than just "content", I am happy. Why? I am not sure. I can think of some reasons. I have given up with what one of my friends once categorized as, "shoulds and coulds". I no longer do things necessarily because of obligation, nor focus on regrets about things never done or accomplished. I know I cannot do anything about them. As to the future, I don't waste a good worry. The future is just - - a hope.

Basic to my attitude, is the fact that currently I am relatively healthy, aside from the area of flexibility. Years ago, my automobile would periodically get a "lube job; I can't. As to sensory faculties, I sense adequately with all of my five senses. I am grateful for living this long, for being granted the gift of watching the progress of my beloved family's lives, for having the capacity to pray and hope for a safer, fairer, and better cherished world. I have indeed been blessed.

Recently, in going through some papers, I came across the following. Although I wrote it about a year ago, it's valid "now".

ALIVE AND WELL

It is Friday evening,
Shortly before I light the Sabbath candles.
I stopped at what I was doing.
I heard myself audibly say,
"I'm so glad to be alive".

It puzzles me.
What made me say that?
It was an overwhelming feeling
of appreciation of where I am,
not physically
but all-embracing.

It's the essence of "good"
gushing from deep down in my guts.
It's almost like
falling in love.

ACKNOWLEDGEMENT

It's done. The project is completed. I would not have reached this point without the input of a number of bright, creative, generous and talented individuals. Each of the following individuals have graciously contributed to this venture. I am profoundly grateful to: Lee Eiferman, writer and gardener, who launched me on this project and pruned the plot; to Jack Eiferman, counselor, for "backing me up" with his sage advice re: appropriate steps; to Loren Eiferman, sculptor, for carving the design; to Fern Fisher, multifaceted craftsman, for her photographic renderings; to Tim Duch, artist and editor, for his artistic depiction and comprehensive editing; to Joe Berlinger, director and documentarian, for what else, but "calling the shots"; to Julia Eiferman, technology guru and advisor re: inclusions and exclusions.

POSTSCRIPT

Although I have acknowledged those who were instrumental in helping me write and complete this opus, there are some others who have impacted my life in significant ways and some only tangentially. But I am grateful to **each** of them for helping to make my past and or current status possible and fulfilling.

To my family:
> My children three: Jack, Leora and Loren and to their spouses: Fern Fisher, Tim Duch and Joe Berlinger. To my grandchildren: Julia, Reva and Bennett Eiferman, Nicholas and Jonah Duch, Sarah and Maya Berlinger. To Hill, Michael and Julie Boss, Ali and David Pflaum, Max Sobel, Freda Wagner and last but not least, Norma Wagner.

To my friends and neighbors:
> Charlotte Balsam, Mira and John Boland, Pearl Deligdish, Diane and Bernie Gissinger, Pat Goldman, Ellen Goldstein, Gloria Greenman, Shirley Horowitz, Peter and Heather Malin, Rochelle and Aaron Polsky, Mitch Rothschild, Irma Schechter,

Marcia Sheiman, Pearl Turk and Cecilia
Williams.

To Riverdalians:
Rochelle Aruti, Harriet Balag, Erica and
Rabbi Joseph Brodie, Margaret Danishevsky,
Joel Einleger and Miriam Westheimer,
Meechal and Chaim Haas, Vivian Kasen,
Rabbi Barry Katz, Sandy Leiman, Ilana and
Baruch Lev, Ruth Licht, Diane Meranus,
Anita Nerwen, Ted and Iris Phillips, Bea
Rosen, Roz and Sam Samuels, Lore Schloss,
Phyllis and Charlie Schulberg, Diane Sharon,
Michael Smith, Ruth Weintraub, and last but
not least, Miriam Young.

LIONS Club

every c

Downtown *

Made in the USA
Middletown, DE
15 March 2015